This Journal Belongs To:

_____

"Traveling leaves you speechless,

then turns you into a storyteller."

— Ibn Battuta

Visit Us
www.enchantedwillowco.com

Date: _____	From: _____	Beginning Mileage: _____
Weather:	To: _____	Ending Mileage: _____
☀ ⛅ ☔ ❄ 🌡 🌡 🎏 ☁	Route Taken: _____	Total Miles Traveled: _____

CAMPGROUND INFORMATION

Name: _____

Address: _____

Phone: _____

Our Rating: ☆ ☆ ☆ ☆ ☆

GPS: _____

Altitude: _____

Cell Service / Carrier: _____

Site # _____ $ _____ ☐ Day ☐ Week ☐ Month

☐ First Visit ☐ Return Visit ☐ Easy Access
☐ Site Level ☐ Back-in ☐ Pull-through
☐ 15 amp ☐ 30 amp ☐ 50 amp
☐ Water ☐ Sewer ☐ Shade ☐ Sun
☐ Paved ☐ Sand / Grass ☐ Gravel
☐ Picnic Table ☐ Fire ring ☐ Trees ☐ Lawn
☐ Patio ☐ Kid Friendly ☐ Pet Friendly
☐ Store ☐ Cafe ☐ Firewood
☐ Ice ☐ Security ☐ Quiet ☐ Noisy

☐ Antenna Reception ☐ Satellite TV ☐ Cable TV
☐ WIFI Available ☐ Free ☐ Fee $ _____

Memberships: _____

Amenities: _____

Location	☺ ☺ ☹	Water Pressure	☺ ☺ ☹
Restrooms	☺ ☺ ☹	Laundry	☺ ☺ ☹
Pool	☺ ☺ ☹	Hot Tub	☺ ☺ ☹

PLACES VISITED / ACTIVITIES: _____
_____
_____
_____

PEOPLE MET / NEW FRIENDS: _____
_____
_____
_____

FOOD, DINING & RESTAURANTS: _____
_____
_____
_____

HIGHLIGHTS / MEMORABLE EVENTS: _____
_____
_____
_____

PLACES TO GO & THINGS TO DO FOR NEXT TIME: _____
_____
_____
_____
_____

NOTES:

Date: _____	From: _____	Beginning Mileage: _____
Weather:	To: _____	Ending Mileage: _____
☀ ⛅ ☔ ❄ 🌡 ❄ 🌬 ☁	Route Taken: _____ _____	Total Miles Traveled: _____

Campground Information

Name: _____

Address: _____

Phone: _____

Our Rating: ☆ ☆ ☆ ☆ ☆

GPS: _____

Altitude: _____

Site # _____ $ _____ ☐ Day ☐ Week ☐ Month

Cell Service / Carrier: _____

☐ First Visit	☐ Return Visit	☐ Easy Access
☐ Site Level	☐ Back-in	☐ Pull-through
☐ 15 amp	☐ 30 amp	☐ 50 amp
☐ Water	☐ Sewer	☐ Shade ☐ Sun
☐ Paved	☐ Sand / Grass	☐ Gravel
☐ Picnic Table	☐ Fire ring	☐ Trees ☐ Lawn
☐ Patio	☐ Kid Friendly	☐ Pet Friendly
☐ Store	☐ Cafe	☐ Firewood
☐ Ice	☐ Security	☐ Quiet ☐ Noisy

☐ Antenna Reception ☐ Satellite TV ☐ Cable TV

☐ WIFI Available ☐ Free ☐ Fee $ _____

Memberships: _____

Amenities: _____

Location	☺ ☺ ☹	Water Pressure	☺ ☺ ☹
Restrooms	☺ ☺ ☹	Laundry	☺ ☺ ☹
Pool	☺ ☺ ☹	Hot Tub	☺ ☺ ☹

Places Visited / Activities:
_____
_____
_____
_____

People Met / New Friends:
_____
_____
_____
_____

Food, Dining & Restaurants:
_____
_____
_____
_____

Highlights / Memorable Events:
_____
_____
_____
_____

Places To Go & Things To Do for Next Time:
_____
_____
_____
_____

NOTES:

Date: _____

Weather:

☀ ⛅ ☂ ❄
🌡 🌡 📢 ☁

From: _____

To: _____

Route Taken: _____

_____

Beginning Mileage: _____

Ending Mileage: _____

Total Miles Traveled: _____

CAMPGROUND INFORMATION

Name: _____

Address: _____

Phone: _____

Site # _____ $ _____ ☐ Day ☐ Week ☐ Month

☐ First Visit   ☐ Return Visit   ☐ Easy Access
☐ Site Level   ☐ Back-in   ☐ Pull-through
☐ 15 amp   ☐ 30 amp   ☐ 50 amp
☐ Water   ☐ Sewer   ☐ Shade   ☐ Sun
☐ Paved   ☐ Sand / Grass   ☐ Gravel
☐ Picnic Table   ☐ Fire ring   ☐ Trees   ☐ Lawn
☐ Patio   ☐ Kid Friendly   ☐ Pet Friendly
☐ Store   ☐ Cafe   ☐ Firewood
☐ Ice   ☐ Security   ☐ Quiet   ☐ Noisy

Our Rating: ☆ ☆ ☆ ☆ ☆

GPS: _____

Altitude: _____

Cell Service / Carrier: _____

☐ Antenna Reception   ☐ Satellite TV   ☐ Cable TV
☐ WIFI Available   ☐ Free   ☐ Fee $ _____

Memberships: _____

Amenities: _____

Location   ☺ ☺ ☹   Water Pressure   ☺ ☺ ☹
Restrooms   ☺ ☺ ☹   Laundry   ☺ ☺ ☹
Pool   ☺ ☺ ☹   Hot Tub   ☺ ☺ ☹

PLACES VISITED / ACTIVITIES: _____

_____

_____

_____

PEOPLE MET / NEW FRIENDS: _____

_____

_____

_____

FOOD, DINING & RESTAURANTS: _____

_____

_____

_____

HIGHLIGHTS / MEMORABLE EVENTS: _____

_____

_____

_____

PLACES TO GO & THINGS TO DO FOR NEXT TIME: _____

_____

_____

_____

_____

NOTES:

Date: _____

Weather:

☀ ⛅ ☔ ❄

🌡 🌡 🚩 ☁

From: _____

To: _____

Route Taken: _____

_____

Beginning Mileage: _____

Ending Mileage: _____

Total Miles Traveled: _____

Campground Information

Name: _____

Address: _____

Phone: _____

Site # _____ $ _____ ☐ Day ☐ Week ☐ Month

☐ First Visit ☐ Return Visit ☐ Easy Access
☐ Site Level ☐ Back-in ☐ Pull-through
☐ 15 amp ☐ 30 amp ☐ 50 amp
☐ Water ☐ Sewer ☐ Shade ☐ Sun
☐ Paved ☐ Sand / Grass ☐ Gravel
☐ Picnic Table ☐ Fire ring ☐ Trees ☐ Lawn
☐ Patio ☐ Kid Friendly ☐ Pet Friendly
☐ Store ☐ Cafe ☐ Firewood
☐ Ice ☐ Security ☐ Quiet ☐ Noisy

Our Rating: ☆ ☆ ☆ ☆ ☆

GPS: _____

Altitude: _____

Cell Service / Carrier: _____

☐ Antenna Reception ☐ Satellite TV ☐ Cable TV
☐ WIFI Available ☐ Free ☐ Fee $ _____

Memberships: _____

Amenities: _____

Location ☺ ☺ ☹   Water Pressure ☺ ☺ ☹
Restrooms ☺ ☺ ☹   Laundry ☺ ☺ ☹
Pool ☺ ☺ ☹   Hot Tub ☺ ☺ ☹

Places Visited / Activities:
_____
_____
_____
_____

People Met / New Friends:
_____
_____
_____
_____

Food, Dining & Restaurants:
_____
_____
_____
_____

Highlights / Memorable Events:
_____
_____
_____
_____

Places To Go & Things To Do for Next Time:
_____
_____
_____
_____

NOTES:

Date: _____

Weather:

☀ ⛅ ☔ ❄
🌡 🌡 📢 ☁

From: _____

To: _____

Route Taken: _____

_____

Beginning Mileage: _____

Ending Mileage: _____

Total Miles Traveled: _____

CAMPGROUND INFORMATION

Name: _____

Address: _____

Phone: _____

Site # _____ $ _____ ☐ Day ☐ Week ☐ Month

☐ First Visit   ☐ Return Visit   ☐ Easy Access
☐ Site Level   ☐ Back-in   ☐ Pull-through
☐ 15 amp   ☐ 30 amp   ☐ 50 amp
☐ Water   ☐ Sewer   ☐ Shade   ☐ Sun
☐ Paved   ☐ Sand / Grass   ☐ Gravel
☐ Picnic Table   ☐ Fire ring   ☐ Trees   ☐ Lawn
☐ Patio   ☐ Kid Friendly   ☐ Pet Friendly
☐ Store   ☐ Cafe   ☐ Firewood
☐ Ice   ☐ Security   ☐ Quiet   ☐ Noisy

Our Rating: ☆ ☆ ☆ ☆ ☆

GPS: _____

Altitude: _____

Cell Service / Carrier: _____

☐ Antenna Reception   ☐ Satellite TV   ☐ Cable TV
☐ WIFI Available   ☐ Free ☐ Fee $ _____

Memberships: _____

Amenities: _____

Location	☺	☻	☹	Water Pressure	☺	☻	☹
Restrooms	☺	☻	☹	Laundry	☺	☻	☹
Pool	☺	☻	☹	Hot Tub	☺	☻	☹

PLACES VISITED / ACTIVITIES: _____

_____

_____

_____

PEOPLE MET / NEW FRIENDS: _____

_____

_____

_____

FOOD, DINING & RESTAURANTS: _____

_____

_____

_____

HIGHLIGHTS / MEMORABLE EVENTS: _____

_____

_____

_____

PLACES TO GO & THINGS TO DO FOR NEXT TIME: _____

_____

_____

_____

_____

NOTES:

Date: _____

Weather:

☀ ☁ ☂ ❄
🌡 🌡 🎐 ☁

From: _____

To: _____

Route Taken: _____

_____

Beginning Mileage:

_____

Ending Mileage:

_____

Total Miles Traveled:

CAMPGROUND INFORMATION

Name: _____

Address: _____

Phone: _____

Site # _____ $ _____ ☐ Day ☐ Week ☐ Month

☐ First Visit ☐ Return Visit ☐ Easy Access
☐ Site Level ☐ Back-in ☐ Pull-through
☐ 15 amp ☐ 30 amp ☐ 50 amp
☐ Water ☐ Sewer ☐ Shade ☐ Sun
☐ Paved ☐ Sand / Grass ☐ Gravel
☐ Picnic Table ☐ Fire ring ☐ Trees ☐ Lawn
☐ Patio ☐ Kid Friendly ☐ Pet Friendly
☐ Store ☐ Cafe ☐ Firewood
☐ Ice ☐ Security ☐ Quiet ☐ Noisy

Our Rating: ☆ ☆ ☆ ☆ ☆

GPS: _____

Altitude: _____

Cell Service / Carrier: _____

☐ Antenna Reception ☐ Satellite TV ☐ Cable TV
☐ WIFI Available ☐ Free ☐ Fee $ _____

Memberships: _____

Amenities: _____

Location   ☺ ☺ ☹   Water Pressure ☺ ☺ ☹
Restrooms   ☺ ☺ ☹   Laundry   ☺ ☺ ☹
Pool   ☺ ☺ ☹   Hot Tub   ☺ ☺ ☹

PLACES VISITED / ACTIVITIES: _____

_____

_____

_____

PEOPLE MET / NEW FRIENDS: _____

_____

_____

_____

FOOD, DINING & RESTAURANTS: _____

_____

_____

_____

HIGHLIGHTS / MEMORABLE EVENTS: _____

_____

_____

_____

PLACES TO GO & THINGS TO DO FOR NEXT TIME: _____

_____

_____

_____

_____

NOTES:

Date: _____

Weather:

☀ ☁ ☂ ❄

🌡 🌡 📢 ☁

From: _____

To: _____

Route Taken: _____

_____

Beginning Mileage: _____

Ending Mileage: _____

Total Miles Traveled: _____

CAMPGROUND INFORMATION

Name: _____

Address: _____

Phone: _____

Site # _____ $ _____ ☐ Day ☐ Week ☐ Month

☐ First Visit   ☐ Return Visit   ☐ Easy Access
☐ Site Level   ☐ Back-in   ☐ Pull-through
☐ 15 amp   ☐ 30 amp   ☐ 50 amp
☐ Water   ☐ Sewer   ☐ Shade   ☐ Sun
☐ Paved   ☐ Sand / Grass   ☐ Gravel
☐ Picnic Table   ☐ Fire ring   ☐ Trees   ☐ Lawn
☐ Patio   ☐ Kid Friendly   ☐ Pet Friendly
☐ Store   ☐ Cafe   ☐ Firewood
☐ Ice   ☐ Security   ☐ Quiet   ☐ Noisy

Our Rating: ☆ ☆ ☆ ☆ ☆

GPS: _____

Altitude: _____

Cell Service / Carrier: _____

☐ Antenna Reception   ☐ Satellite TV   ☐ Cable TV
☐ WIFI Available   ☐ Free   ☐ Fee $ _____

Memberships: _____

Amenities: _____

Location	☺	☺	☹	Water Pressure	☺	☺	☹
Restrooms	☺	☺	☹	Laundry	☺	☺	☹
Pool	☺	☺	☹	Hot Tub	☺	☺	☹

PLACES VISITED / ACTIVITIES: _____

_____
_____
_____

PEOPLE MET / NEW FRIENDS: _____

_____
_____
_____

FOOD, DINING & RESTAURANTS: _____

_____
_____
_____

HIGHLIGHTS / MEMORABLE EVENTS: _____

_____
_____
_____

PLACES TO GO & THINGS TO DO FOR NEXT TIME: _____

_____
_____
_____
_____

NOTES:

Date: _____

Weather:

☀ ⛅ ☂ ❄

🌡 🌡 🎏 ☁

From: _____

To: _____

Route Taken: _____

_____

Beginning Mileage: _____

Ending Mileage: _____

Total Miles Traveled: _____

CAMPGROUND INFORMATION

Name: _____

Address: _____

Phone: _____

Site # _____ $ _____ ☐ Day ☐ Week ☐ Month

☐ First Visit   ☐ Return Visit   ☐ Easy Access
☐ Site Level   ☐ Back-in   ☐ Pull-through
☐ 15 amp   ☐ 30 amp   ☐ 50 amp
☐ Water   ☐ Sewer   ☐ Shade   ☐ Sun
☐ Paved   ☐ Sand / Grass   ☐ Gravel
☐ Picnic Table   ☐ Fire ring   ☐ Trees   ☐ Lawn
☐ Patio   ☐ Kid Friendly   ☐ Pet Friendly
☐ Store   ☐ Cafe   ☐ Firewood
☐ Ice   ☐ Security   ☐ Quiet   ☐ Noisy

Our Rating: ☆ ☆ ☆ ☆ ☆

GPS: _____

Altitude: _____

Cell Service / Carrier: _____

☐ Antenna Reception   ☐ Satellite TV   ☐ Cable TV
☐ WIFI Available   ☐ Free ☐ Fee $ _____

Memberships: _____

Amenities: _____

Location	🙂	😐	🙁	Water Pressure	🙂	😐	🙁
Restrooms	🙂	😐	🙁	Laundry	🙂	😐	🙁
Pool	🙂	😐	🙁	Hot Tub	🙂	😐	🙁

PLACES VISITED / ACTIVITIES: _____

_____
_____
_____

PEOPLE MET / NEW FRIENDS: _____

_____
_____
_____

FOOD, DINING & RESTAURANTS: _____

_____
_____
_____

HIGHLIGHTS / MEMORABLE EVENTS: _____

_____
_____
_____

PLACES TO GO & THINGS TO DO FOR NEXT TIME: _____

_____
_____
_____
_____

NOTES:

Date: _____

Weather:

☀ ⛅ ☔ ❄
🌡 🌡 🚩 ☁

From: _____

To: _____

Route Taken: _____

_____

Beginning Mileage: _____

Ending Mileage: _____

Total Miles Traveled: _____

CAMPGROUND INFORMATION

Name: _____

Address: _____

Phone: _____

Site # _____ $ _____ ☐ Day ☐ Week ☐ Month

☐ First Visit ☐ Return Visit ☐ Easy Access
☐ Site Level ☐ Back-in ☐ Pull-through
☐ 15 amp ☐ 30 amp ☐ 50 amp
☐ Water ☐ Sewer ☐ Shade ☐ Sun
☐ Paved ☐ Sand / Grass ☐ Gravel
☐ Picnic Table ☐ Fire ring ☐ Trees ☐ Lawn
☐ Patio ☐ Kid Friendly ☐ Pet Friendly
☐ Store ☐ Cafe ☐ Firewood
☐ Ice ☐ Security ☐ Quiet ☐ Noisy

Our Rating: ☆ ☆ ☆ ☆ ☆

GPS: _____

Altitude: _____

Cell Service / Carrier: _____

☐ Antenna Reception ☐ Satellite TV ☐ Cable TV
☐ WIFI Available ☐ Free ☐ Fee $ _____

Memberships: _____

Amenities: _____

Location	☺	☺	☹	Water Pressure	☺	☺	☹
Restrooms	☺	☺	☹	Laundry	☺	☺	☹
Pool	☺	☺	☹	Hot Tub	☺	☺	☹

PLACES VISITED / ACTIVITIES: _____

_____

_____

_____

PEOPLE MET / NEW FRIENDS: _____

_____

_____

_____

FOOD, DINING & RESTAURANTS: _____

_____

_____

_____

HIGHLIGHTS / MEMORABLE EVENTS: _____

_____

_____

_____

PLACES TO GO & THINGS TO DO FOR NEXT TIME: _____

_____

_____

_____

_____

NOTES:

Date: _____

Weather:

From: _____

To: _____

Route Taken: _____

_____

Beginning Mileage:
_____

Ending Mileage:
_____

Total Miles Traveled:
_____

CAMPGROUND INFORMATION

Name: _____

Address: _____

Phone: _____

Site # _____ $ _____ ☐ Day ☐ Week ☐ Month

☐ First Visit   ☐ Return Visit   ☐ Easy Access
☐ Site Level   ☐ Back-in   ☐ Pull-through
☐ 15 amp   ☐ 30 amp   ☐ 50 amp
☐ Water   ☐ Sewer   ☐ Shade   ☐ Sun
☐ Paved   ☐ Sand / Grass   ☐ Gravel
☐ Picnic Table   ☐ Fire ring   ☐ Trees   ☐ Lawn
☐ Patio   ☐ Kid Friendly   ☐ Pet Friendly
☐ Store   ☐ Cafe   ☐ Firewood
☐ Ice   ☐ Security   ☐ Quiet   ☐ Noisy

Our Rating: ☆ ☆ ☆ ☆ ☆

GPS: _____

Altitude: _____

Cell Service / Carrier: _____

☐ Antenna Reception   ☐ Satellite TV   ☐ Cable TV
☐ WIFI Available   ☐ Free   ☐ Fee $ _____

Memberships: _____

Amenities: _____

Location	☺	☺	☹	Water Pressure	☺	☺	☹
Restrooms	☺	☺	☹	Laundry	☺	☺	☹
Pool	☺	☺	☹	Hot Tub	☺	☺	☹

PLACES VISITED / ACTIVITIES: _____

_____
_____
_____

PEOPLE MET / NEW FRIENDS: _____

_____
_____
_____

FOOD, DINING & RESTAURANTS: _____

_____
_____
_____

HIGHLIGHTS / MEMORABLE EVENTS: _____

_____
_____
_____

PLACES TO GO & THINGS TO DO FOR NEXT TIME: _____

_____
_____
_____
_____

NOTES:

Date:	From:	Beginning Mileage:
Weather:	To:	Ending Mileage:
	Route Taken:	Total Miles Traveled:

CAMPGROUND INFORMATION

Name: _____

Address: _____

Phone: _____

Our Rating: ☆ ☆ ☆ ☆ ☆

GPS: _____

Altitude: _____

Site # _____ $ _____ ☐ Day ☐ Week ☐ Month

Cell Service / Carrier: _____

☐ First Visit	☐ Return Visit	☐ Easy Access
☐ Site Level	☐ Back-in	☐ Pull-through
☐ 15 amp	☐ 30 amp	☐ 50 amp
☐ Water	☐ Sewer	☐ Shade ☐ Sun
☐ Paved	☐ Sand / Grass	☐ Gravel
☐ Picnic Table	☐ Fire ring	☐ Trees ☐ Lawn
☐ Patio	☐ Kid Friendly	☐ Pet Friendly
☐ Store	☐ Cafe	☐ Firewood
☐ Ice	☐ Security	☐ Quiet ☐ Noisy

☐ Antenna Reception ☐ Satellite TV ☐ Cable TV
☐ WIFI Available ☐ Free ☐ Fee $ _____

Memberships: _____

Amenities: _____

Location	☺ ☺ ☹	Water Pressure	☺ ☺ ☹
Restrooms	☺ ☺ ☹	Laundry	☺ ☺ ☹
Pool	☺ ☺ ☹	Hot Tub	☺ ☺ ☹

PLACES VISITED / ACTIVITIES: _____

_____

_____

_____

PEOPLE MET / NEW FRIENDS: _____

_____

_____

_____

FOOD, DINING & RESTAURANTS: _____

_____

_____

_____

HIGHLIGHTS / MEMORABLE EVENTS: _____

_____

_____

_____

PLACES TO GO & THINGS TO DO FOR NEXT TIME: _____

_____

_____

_____

_____

NOTES:

Date: _____	From: _____	Beginning Mileage:
Weather:	To: _____	_____
	Route Taken: _____	Ending Mileage:
	_____	Total Miles Traveled:

CAMPGROUND INFORMATION

Name: _____

Address: _____

Phone: _____

Site # _____ $ _____ ☐ Day ☐ Week ☐ Month

☐ First Visit   ☐ Return Visit   ☐ Easy Access
☐ Site Level   ☐ Back-in   ☐ Pull-through
☐ 15 amp   ☐ 30 amp   ☐ 50 amp
☐ Water   ☐ Sewer   ☐ Shade   ☐ Sun
☐ Paved   ☐ Sand / Grass   ☐ Gravel
☐ Picnic Table   ☐ Fire ring   ☐ Trees   ☐ Lawn
☐ Patio   ☐ Kid Friendly   ☐ Pet Friendly
☐ Store   ☐ Cafe   ☐ Firewood
☐ Ice   ☐ Security   ☐ Quiet   ☐ Noisy

Our Rating: ☆ ☆ ☆ ☆ ☆

GPS: _____

Altitude: _____

Cell Service / Carrier: _____

☐ Antenna Reception   ☐ Satellite TV   ☐ Cable TV
☐ WIFI Available   ☐ Free ☐ Fee $ _____

Memberships: _____

Amenities: _____

Location	☺ ☺ ☹	Water Pressure	☺ ☺ ☹
Restrooms	☺ ☺ ☹	Laundry	☺ ☺ ☹
Pool	☺ ☺ ☹	Hot Tub	☺ ☺ ☹

PLACES VISITED / ACTIVITIES: _____

_____
_____
_____

PEOPLE MET / NEW FRIENDS: _____

_____
_____
_____

FOOD, DINING & RESTAURANTS: _____

_____
_____
_____

HIGHLIGHTS / MEMORABLE EVENTS: _____

_____
_____
_____

PLACES TO GO & THINGS TO DO FOR NEXT TIME: _____

_____
_____
_____
_____

NOTES:

Date: _____

Weather:

☀ ☁ ☔ ❄

🌡 🌡 🌬 ☁

From: _____

To: _____

Route Taken: _____

_____

Beginning Mileage:

_____

Ending Mileage:

_____

Total Miles Traveled:

_____

Name: _____

Address: _____

Phone: _____

Site # _____ $ _____ ☐ Day ☐ Week ☐ Month

☐ First Visit   ☐ Return Visit   ☐ Easy Access
☐ Site Level   ☐ Back-in   ☐ Pull-through
☐ 15 amp   ☐ 30 amp   ☐ 50 amp
☐ Water   ☐ Sewer   ☐ Shade   ☐ Sun
☐ Paved   ☐ Sand / Grass   ☐ Gravel
☐ Picnic Table   ☐ Fire ring   ☐ Trees   ☐ Lawn
☐ Patio   ☐ Kid Friendly   ☐ Pet Friendly
☐ Store   ☐ Cafe   ☐ Firewood
☐ Ice   ☐ Security   ☐ Quiet   ☐ Noisy

Our Rating: ☆ ☆ ☆ ☆ ☆

GPS: _____

Altitude: _____

Cell Service / Carrier: _____

☐ Antenna Reception   ☐ Satellite TV   ☐ Cable TV
☐ WIFI Available   ☐ Free ☐ Fee $ _____

Memberships: _____

Amenities: _____

Location	☺	😐	☹	Water Pressure	☺	😐	☹
Restrooms	☺	😐	☹	Laundry	☺	😐	☹
Pool	☺	😐	☹	Hot Tub	☺	😐	☹

PLACES VISITED / ACTIVITIES: _____

_____

_____

_____

PEOPLE MET / NEW FRIENDS: _____

_____

_____

_____

FOOD, DINING & RESTAURANTS: _____

_____

_____

_____

HIGHLIGHTS / MEMORABLE EVENTS: _____

_____

_____

_____

PLACES TO GO & THINGS TO DO FOR NEXT TIME: _____

_____

_____

_____

_____

NOTES:

Date: _____

Weather:

☀ ⛅ ☔ ❄

🌡 ❄ 🎏 ☁

From: _____

To: _____

Route Taken: _____

_____

Beginning Mileage: _____

Ending Mileage: _____

Total Miles Traveled: _____

CAMPGROUND INFORMATION

Name: _____

Address: _____

Phone: _____

Site # _____ $ _____ ☐ Day ☐ Week ☐ Month

☐ First Visit   ☐ Return Visit   ☐ Easy Access
☐ Site Level   ☐ Back-in   ☐ Pull-through
☐ 15 amp   ☐ 30 amp   ☐ 50 amp
☐ Water   ☐ Sewer   ☐ Shade   ☐ Sun
☐ Paved   ☐ Sand / Grass   ☐ Gravel
☐ Picnic Table   ☐ Fire ring   ☐ Trees   ☐ Lawn
☐ Patio   ☐ Kid Friendly   ☐ Pet Friendly
☐ Store   ☐ Cafe   ☐ Firewood
☐ Ice   ☐ Security   ☐ Quiet   ☐ Noisy

Our Rating: ☆ ☆ ☆ ☆ ☆

GPS: _____

Altitude: _____

Cell Service / Carrier: _____

☐ Antenna Reception   ☐ Satellite TV   ☐ Cable TV
☐ WIFI Available   ☐ Free   ☐ Fee $ _____

Memberships: _____

Amenities: _____

Location	☺	☺	☹	Water Pressure	☺	☺	☹
Restrooms	☺	☺	☹	Laundry	☺	☺	☹
Pool	☺	☺	☹	Hot Tub	☺	☺	☹

PLACES VISITED / ACTIVITIES:
_____
_____
_____
_____

PEOPLE MET / NEW FRIENDS:
_____
_____
_____
_____

FOOD, DINING & RESTAURANTS:
_____
_____
_____
_____

HIGHLIGHTS / MEMORABLE EVENTS:
_____
_____
_____
_____

PLACES TO GO & THINGS TO DO FOR NEXT TIME:
_____
_____
_____
_____

NOTES:

Date: _____

Weather:

☀ ☁ ☂ ❄

🌡 🌡 📢 ☁

From: _____

To: _____

Route Taken: _____

_____

Beginning Mileage: _____

Ending Mileage: _____

Total Miles Traveled: _____

CAMPGROUND INFORMATION

Name: _____

Address: _____

Phone: _____

Site # _____ $ _____ ☐ Day ☐ Week ☐ Month

☐ First Visit ☐ Return Visit ☐ Easy Access
☐ Site Level ☐ Back-in ☐ Pull-through
☐ 15 amp ☐ 30 amp ☐ 50 amp
☐ Water ☐ Sewer ☐ Shade ☐ Sun
☐ Paved ☐ Sand / Grass ☐ Gravel
☐ Picnic Table ☐ Fire ring ☐ Trees ☐ Lawn
☐ Patio ☐ Kid Friendly ☐ Pet Friendly
☐ Store ☐ Cafe ☐ Firewood
☐ Ice ☐ Security ☐ Quiet ☐ Noisy

Our Rating: ☆ ☆ ☆ ☆ ☆

GPS: _____

Altitude: _____

Cell Service / Carrier: _____

☐ Antenna Reception ☐ Satellite TV ☐ Cable TV
☐ WIFI Available ☐ Free ☐ Fee $ _____

Memberships: _____

Amenities: _____

Location	☺	😐	☹	Water Pressure	☺	😐	☹
Restrooms	☺	😐	☹	Laundry	☺	😐	☹
Pool	☺	😐	☹	Hot Tub	☺	😐	☹

PLACES VISITED / ACTIVITIES: _____
_____
_____
_____

PEOPLE MET / NEW FRIENDS: _____
_____
_____
_____

FOOD, DINING & RESTAURANTS: _____
_____
_____
_____

HIGHLIGHTS / MEMORABLE EVENTS: _____
_____
_____
_____

PLACES TO GO & THINGS TO DO FOR NEXT TIME: _____
_____
_____
_____
_____

NOTES:

Date: _____

Weather:

☀ ⛅ ☂ ❄
🌡 🌡 🚩 ☁

From: _____

To: _____

Route Taken: _____
_____

Beginning Mileage:
_____

Ending Mileage:
_____

Total Miles Traveled:
_____

Campground Information

Name: _____

Address: _____

Phone: _____

Site # _____ $ _____ ☐ Day ☐ Week ☐ Month

☐ First Visit	☐ Return Visit	☐ Easy Access
☐ Site Level	☐ Back-in	☐ Pull-through
☐ 15 amp	☐ 30 amp	☐ 50 amp
☐ Water	☐ Sewer	☐ Shade ☐ Sun
☐ Paved	☐ Sand / Grass	☐ Gravel
☐ Picnic Table	☐ Fire ring	☐ Trees ☐ Lawn
☐ Patio	☐ Kid Friendly	☐ Pet Friendly
☐ Store	☐ Cafe	☐ Firewood
☐ Ice	☐ Security	☐ Quiet ☐ Noisy

Our Rating: ☆ ☆ ☆ ☆ ☆

GPS: _____

Altitude: _____

Cell Service / Carrier: _____

☐ Antenna Reception   ☐ Satellite TV   ☐ Cable TV
☐ WIFI Available   ☐ Free ☐ Fee $ _____

Memberships: _____

Amenities: _____

	☺	😐	☹		☺	😐	☹
Location	☺	😐	☹	Water Pressure	☺	😐	☹
Restrooms	☺	😐	☹	Laundry	☺	😐	☹
Pool	☺	😐	☹	Hot Tub	☺	😐	☹

Places Visited / Activities: _____
_____
_____
_____

People Met / New Friends: _____
_____
_____
_____

Food, Dining & Restaurants: _____
_____
_____
_____
_____

Highlights / Memorable Events: _____
_____
_____
_____
_____

Places To Go & Things To Do for Next Time: _____
_____
_____
_____
_____

NOTES:

Date: _____

Weather:

☀ ☁ ☂ ❄

🌡 🌡 📢 ☁

From: _____

To: _____

Route Taken: _____

_____

Beginning Mileage:

_____

Ending Mileage:

_____

Total Miles Traveled:

_____

Campground Information

Name: _____

Address: _____

Phone: _____

Site # _____ $ _____ ☐ Day ☐ Week ☐ Month

☐ First Visit   ☐ Return Visit   ☐ Easy Access
☐ Site Level   ☐ Back-in   ☐ Pull-through
☐ 15 amp   ☐ 30 amp   ☐ 50 amp
☐ Water   ☐ Sewer   ☐ Shade   ☐ Sun
☐ Paved   ☐ Sand / Grass   ☐ Gravel
☐ Picnic Table   ☐ Fire ring   ☐ Trees   ☐ Lawn
☐ Patio   ☐ Kid Friendly   ☐ Pet Friendly
☐ Store   ☐ Cafe   ☐ Firewood
☐ Ice   ☐ Security   ☐ Quiet   ☐ Noisy

Our Rating: ☆ ☆ ☆ ☆ ☆

GPS: _____

Altitude: _____

Cell Service / Carrier: _____

☐ Antenna Reception   ☐ Satellite TV   ☐ Cable TV
☐ WIFI Available   ☐ Free   ☐ Fee $ _____

Memberships: _____

Amenities: _____

Location	☺	☻	☹	Water Pressure	☺	☻	☹
Restrooms	☺	☻	☹	Laundry	☺	☻	☹
Pool	☺	☻	☹	Hot Tub	☺	☻	☹

Places Visited / Activities: _____

_____
_____
_____

People Met / New Friends: _____

_____
_____
_____

Food, Dining & Restaurants: _____

_____
_____
_____

Highlights / Memorable Events: _____

_____
_____
_____

Places To Go & Things To Do for Next Time: _____

_____
_____
_____
_____

NOTES:

Date: _____

Weather:

☀ ⛅ ☂ ❄
🌡 🌡 🔦 ☁

From: _____

To: _____

Route Taken: _____

_____

Beginning Mileage: _____

Ending Mileage: _____

Total Miles Traveled: _____

CAMPGROUND INFORMATION

Name: _____

Address: _____

Phone: _____

Site # _____ $ _____ ☐ Day ☐ Week ☐ Month

☐ First Visit ☐ Return Visit ☐ Easy Access
☐ Site Level ☐ Back-in ☐ Pull-through
☐ 15 amp ☐ 30 amp ☐ 50 amp
☐ Water ☐ Sewer ☐ Shade ☐ Sun
☐ Paved ☐ Sand / Grass ☐ Gravel
☐ Picnic Table ☐ Fire ring ☐ Trees ☐ Lawn
☐ Patio ☐ Kid Friendly ☐ Pet Friendly
☐ Store ☐ Cafe ☐ Firewood
☐ Ice ☐ Security ☐ Quiet ☐ Noisy

Our Rating: ☆ ☆ ☆ ☆ ☆

GPS: _____

Altitude: _____

Cell Service / Carrier: _____

☐ Antenna Reception ☐ Satellite TV ☐ Cable TV
☐ WIFI Available ☐ Free ☐ Fee $ _____

Memberships: _____

Amenities: _____

Location	☺	☻	☹	Water Pressure	☺	☻	☹
Restrooms	☺	☻	☹	Laundry	☺	☻	☹
Pool	☺	☻	☹	Hot Tub	☺	☻	☹

PLACES VISITED / ACTIVITIES: _____

_____

_____

_____

PEOPLE MET / NEW FRIENDS: _____

_____

_____

_____

FOOD, DINING & RESTAURANTS: _____

_____

_____

_____

HIGHLIGHTS / MEMORABLE EVENTS: _____

_____

_____

_____

PLACES TO GO & THINGS TO DO FOR NEXT TIME: _____

_____

_____

_____

_____

NOTES:

Date: _____

Weather:

From: _____

To: _____

Route Taken: _____

_____

Beginning Mileage: _____

Ending Mileage: _____

Total Miles Traveled: _____

CAMPGROUND INFORMATION

Name: _____

Address: _____

Phone: _____

Site # _____ $ _____ ☐ Day ☐ Week ☐ Month

☐ First Visit
☐ Site Level
☐ 15 amp
☐ Water
☐ Paved
☐ Picnic Table
☐ Patio
☐ Store
☐ Ice

☐ Return Visit
☐ Back-in
☐ 30 amp
☐ Sewer
☐ Sand / Grass
☐ Fire ring
☐ Kid Friendly
☐ Cafe
☐ Security

☐ Easy Access
☐ Pull-through
☐ 50 amp
☐ Shade ☐ Sun
☐ Gravel
☐ Trees ☐ Lawn
☐ Pet Friendly
☐ Firewood
☐ Quiet ☐ Noisy

Our Rating: ☆ ☆ ☆ ☆ ☆

GPS: _____

Altitude: _____

Cell Service / Carrier: _____

☐ Antenna Reception   ☐ Satellite TV   ☐ Cable TV
☐ WIFI Available   ☐ Free ☐ Fee $ _____

Memberships: _____

Amenities: _____

Location	☺	☺	☹	Water Pressure	☺	☺	☹
Restrooms	☺	☺	☹	Laundry	☺	☺	☹
Pool	☺	☺	☹	Hot Tub	☺	☺	☹

PLACES VISITED / ACTIVITIES: _____

_____

_____

_____

PEOPLE MET / NEW FRIENDS: _____

_____

_____

_____

FOOD, DINING & RESTAURANTS: _____

_____

_____

_____

_____

HIGHLIGHTS / MEMORABLE EVENTS: _____

_____

_____

_____

PLACES TO GO & THINGS TO DO FOR NEXT TIME: _____

_____

_____

_____

_____

NOTES:

Date: _____

Weather:

From: _____

To: _____

Route Taken: _____

_____

Beginning Mileage: _____

Ending Mileage: _____

Total Miles Traveled: _____

CAMPGROUND INFORMATION

Name: _____

Address: _____

Phone: _____

Site # _____ $ _____

- [ ] First Visit
- [ ] Site Level
- [ ] 15 amp
- [ ] Water
- [ ] Paved
- [ ] Picnic Table
- [ ] Patio
- [ ] Store
- [ ] Ice

- [ ] Return Visit
- [ ] Back-in
- [ ] 30 amp
- [ ] Sewer
- [ ] Sand / Grass
- [ ] Fire ring
- [ ] Kid Friendly
- [ ] Cafe
- [ ] Security

- [ ] Easy Access
- [ ] Pull-through
- [ ] 50 amp
- [ ] Shade
- [ ] Gravel
- [ ] Trees
- [ ] Pet Friendly
- [ ] Firewood
- [ ] Quiet

- [ ] Day - [ ] Week - [ ] Month

- [ ] Sun
- [ ] Lawn
- [ ] Noisy

Our Rating: ☆ ☆ ☆ ☆ ☆

GPS: _____

Altitude: _____

Cell Service / Carrier: _____

- [ ] Antenna Reception
- [ ] WIFI Available

- [ ] Satellite TV
- [ ] Free

- [ ] Cable TV
- [ ] Fee $ _____

Memberships: _____

Amenities: _____

Location	☺	☺	☹	Water Pressure	☺	☺	☹
Restrooms	☺	☺	☹	Laundry	☺	☺	☹
Pool	☺	☺	☹	Hot Tub	☺	☺	☹

PLACES VISITED / ACTIVITIES: _____

_____

_____

_____

PEOPLE MET / NEW FRIENDS: _____

_____

_____

_____

FOOD, DINING & RESTAURANTS: _____

_____

_____

_____

HIGHLIGHTS / MEMORABLE EVENTS: _____

_____

_____

_____

PLACES TO GO & THINGS TO DO FOR NEXT TIME: _____

_____

_____

_____

_____

NOTES:

Date: _____

Weather:

☀ ☁ ☂ ❄

🌡 🌡 📣 ☁

From: _____

To: _____

Route Taken: _____

_____

Beginning Mileage:
_____

Ending Mileage:
_____

Total Miles Traveled:
_____

CAMPGROUND INFORMATION

Name: _____

Address: _____

Phone: _____

Site # _____ $ _____

☐ First Visit ☐ Return Visit ☐ Easy Access
☐ Site Level ☐ Back-in ☐ Pull-through
☐ 15 amp ☐ 30 amp ☐ 50 amp
☐ Water ☐ Sewer ☐ Shade ☐ Sun
☐ Paved ☐ Sand / Grass ☐ Gravel
☐ Picnic Table ☐ Fire ring ☐ Trees ☐ Lawn
☐ Patio ☐ Kid Friendly ☐ Pet Friendly
☐ Store ☐ Cafe ☐ Firewood
☐ Ice ☐ Security ☐ Quiet ☐ Noisy

Our Rating: ☆ ☆ ☆ ☆ ☆

GPS: _____

Altitude: _____

Cell Service / Carrier: _____

☐ Antenna Reception ☐ Satellite TV ☐ Cable TV
☐ WIFI Available ☐ Free ☐ Fee $ _____

Memberships: _____

Amenities: _____

Location	☺	☺	☹	Water Pressure	☺	☺	☹
Restrooms	☺	☺	☹	Laundry	☺	☺	☹
Pool	☺	☺	☹	Hot Tub	☺	☺	☹

PLACES VISITED / ACTIVITIES: _____

_____
_____
_____

PEOPLE MET / NEW FRIENDS: _____

_____
_____
_____

FOOD, DINING & RESTAURANTS: _____

_____
_____
_____

HIGHLIGHTS / MEMORABLE EVENTS: _____

_____
_____
_____

PLACES TO GO & THINGS TO DO FOR NEXT TIME: _____

_____
_____
_____
_____

NOTES:

Date: _____

Weather:

☀ ⛅ ☂ ❄
🌡 ❄ 🎐 ☁

From: _____

To: _____

Route Taken: _____

_____

Beginning Mileage: _____

Ending Mileage: _____

Total Miles Traveled: _____

CAMPGROUND INFORMATION

Name: _____

Address: _____

Phone: _____

Site # _____ $ _____ ☐ Day ☐ Week ☐ Month

☐ First Visit   ☐ Return Visit   ☐ Easy Access
☐ Site Level   ☐ Back-in   ☐ Pull-through
☐ 15 amp   ☐ 30 amp   ☐ 50 amp
☐ Water   ☐ Sewer   ☐ Shade   ☐ Sun
☐ Paved   ☐ Sand / Grass   ☐ Gravel
☐ Picnic Table   ☐ Fire ring   ☐ Trees   ☐ Lawn
☐ Patio   ☐ Kid Friendly   ☐ Pet Friendly
☐ Store   ☐ Cafe   ☐ Firewood
☐ Ice   ☐ Security   ☐ Quiet   ☐ Noisy

Our Rating: ☆ ☆ ☆ ☆ ☆

GPS: _____

Altitude: _____

Cell Service / Carrier: _____

☐ Antenna Reception   ☐ Satellite TV   ☐ Cable TV
☐ WIFI Available   ☐ Free ☐ Fee $ _____

Memberships: _____

Amenities: _____

Location	☺	☻	☹	Water Pressure	☺	☻	☹
Restrooms	☺	☻	☹	Laundry	☺	☻	☹
Pool	☺	☻	☹	Hot Tub	☺	☻	☹

PLACES VISITED / ACTIVITIES: _____

_____

_____

_____

PEOPLE MET / NEW FRIENDS: _____

_____

_____

_____

FOOD, DINING & RESTAURANTS: _____

_____

_____

_____

HIGHLIGHTS / MEMORABLE EVENTS: _____

_____

_____

_____

PLACES TO GO & THINGS TO DO FOR NEXT TIME: _____

_____

_____

_____

_____

NOTES:

Date: _____

Weather:

From: _____

To: _____

Route Taken: _____

_____

Beginning Mileage: _____

Ending Mileage: _____

Total Miles Traveled: _____

CAMPGROUND INFORMATION

Name: _____

Address: _____

Phone: _____

Our Rating: ☆ ☆ ☆ ☆ ☆

GPS: _____

Altitude: _____

Cell Service / Carrier: _____

Site # _____ $ _____ ☐ Day ☐ Week ☐ Month

☐ First Visit ☐ Return Visit ☐ Easy Access
☐ Site Level ☐ Back-in ☐ Pull-through
☐ 15 amp ☐ 30 amp ☐ 50 amp
☐ Water ☐ Sewer ☐ Shade ☐ Sun
☐ Paved ☐ Sand / Grass ☐ Gravel
☐ Picnic Table ☐ Fire ring ☐ Trees ☐ Lawn
☐ Patio ☐ Kid Friendly ☐ Pet Friendly
☐ Store ☐ Cafe ☐ Firewood
☐ Ice ☐ Security ☐ Quiet ☐ Noisy

☐ Antenna Reception ☐ Satellite TV ☐ Cable TV
☐ WIFI Available ☐ Free ☐ Fee $ _____

Memberships: _____

Amenities: _____

Location	☺	😐	☹	Water Pressure	☺	😐	☹
Restrooms	☺	😐	☹	Laundry	☺	😐	☹
Pool	☺	😐	☹	Hot Tub	☺	😐	☹

PLACES VISITED / ACTIVITIES: _____

_____

_____

_____

PEOPLE MET / NEW FRIENDS: _____

_____

_____

_____

FOOD, DINING & RESTAURANTS: _____

_____

_____

_____

HIGHLIGHTS / MEMORABLE EVENTS: _____

_____

_____

_____

PLACES TO GO & THINGS TO DO FOR NEXT TIME: _____

_____

_____

_____

_____

NOTES:

Date: _____	From: _____	Beginning Mileage: _____
Weather:	To: _____	Ending Mileage: _____
☀ ⛅ ☂ ❄ 🌡 🌡 🚩 ☁	Route Taken: _____	Total Miles Traveled: _____

Campground Information

Name: _____

Address: _____

Phone: _____

Site # _____ **$** _____ ☐ Day ☐ Week ☐ Month

☐ First Visit ☐ Return Visit ☐ Easy Access
☐ Site Level ☐ Back-in ☐ Pull-through
☐ 15 amp ☐ 30 amp ☐ 50 amp
☐ Water ☐ Sewer ☐ Shade ☐ Sun
☐ Paved ☐ Sand / Grass ☐ Gravel
☐ Picnic Table ☐ Fire ring ☐ Trees ☐ Lawn
☐ Patio ☐ Kid Friendly ☐ Pet Friendly
☐ Store ☐ Cafe ☐ Firewood
☐ Ice ☐ Security ☐ Quiet ☐ Noisy

Our Rating: ☆ ☆ ☆ ☆ ☆

GPS: _____

Altitude: _____

Cell Service / Carrier: _____

☐ Antenna Reception ☐ Satellite TV ☐ Cable TV
☐ WIFI Available ☐ Free ☐ Fee $ _____

Memberships: _____

Amenities: _____

Location	☺	😐	☹	Water Pressure	☺	😐	☹
Restrooms	☺	😐	☹	Laundry	☺	😐	☹
Pool	☺	😐	☹	Hot Tub	☺	😐	☹

Places Visited / Activities: _____

_____

_____

_____

People Met / New Friends: _____

_____

_____

_____

Food, Dining & Restaurants: _____

_____

_____

_____

Highlights / Memorable Events: _____

_____

_____

_____

Places To Go & Things To Do for Next Time: _____

_____

_____

_____

_____

NOTES:

Date: _____	From: _____	Beginning Mileage: _____
Weather:	To: _____	Ending Mileage: _____
☀ ☁ ☂ ❄ 🌡 🌡 📣 ☁	Route Taken: _____ _____	Total Miles Traveled: _____

CAMPGROUND INFORMATION

Name: _____

Address: _____

Phone: _____

Our Rating: ☆ ☆ ☆ ☆ ☆

GPS: _____

Altitude: _____

Site # _____ $ _____ ☐ Day ☐ Week ☐ Month

Cell Service / Carrier: _____

☐ First Visit	☐ Return Visit	☐ Easy Access
☐ Site Level	☐ Back-in	☐ Pull-through
☐ 15 amp	☐ 30 amp	☐ 50 amp
☐ Water	☐ Sewer	☐ Shade ☐ Sun
☐ Paved	☐ Sand / Grass	☐ Gravel
☐ Picnic Table	☐ Fire ring	☐ Trees ☐ Lawn
☐ Patio	☐ Kid Friendly	☐ Pet Friendly
☐ Store	☐ Cafe	☐ Firewood
☐ Ice	☐ Security	☐ Quiet ☐ Noisy

☐ Antenna Reception   ☐ Satellite TV   ☐ Cable TV
☐ WIFI Available   ☐ Free   ☐ Fee $ _____

Memberships: _____

Amenities: _____

Location	☺ ☹	Water Pressure	☺ ☹
Restrooms	☺ ☹	Laundry	☺ ☹
Pool	☺ ☹	Hot Tub	☺ ☹

PLACES VISITED / ACTIVITIES:
_____
_____
_____
_____

PEOPLE MET / NEW FRIENDS:
_____
_____
_____
_____

FOOD, DINING & RESTAURANTS:
_____
_____
_____
_____

HIGHLIGHTS / MEMORABLE EVENTS:
_____
_____
_____
_____

PLACES TO GO & THINGS TO DO FOR NEXT TIME:
_____
_____
_____
_____

NOTES:

Date: _____	From: _____	Beginning Mileage:
	To: _____	_____
Weather:		Ending Mileage:
☀ ⛅ ☂ ❄	Route Taken: _____	_____
🌡 ❄ 🎐 ☁	_____	Total Miles Traveled:

CAMPGROUND INFORMATION

Name: _____   Our Rating: ☆ ☆ ☆ ☆ ☆

Address: _____   GPS: _____

Phone: _____   Altitude: _____

Site # _____ $ _____ ☐ Day ☐ Week ☐ Month   Cell Service / Carrier: _____

☐ First Visit	☐ Return Visit	☐ Easy Access		☐ Antenna Reception	☐ Satellite TV	☐ Cable TV
☐ Site Level	☐ Back-in	☐ Pull-through		☐ WIFI Available	☐ Free ☐ Fee $ _____	
☐ 15 amp	☐ 30 amp	☐ 50 amp		Memberships: _____		
☐ Water	☐ Sewer	☐ Shade	☐ Sun	Amenities: _____		
☐ Paved	☐ Sand / Grass	☐ Gravel				
☐ Picnic Table	☐ Fire ring	☐ Trees	☐ Lawn	Location ☺ ☺ ☹	Water Pressure	☺ ☺ ☹
☐ Patio	☐ Kid Friendly	☐ Pet Friendly		Restrooms ☺ ☺ ☹	Laundry	☺ ☺ ☹
☐ Store	☐ Cafe	☐ Firewood		Pool ☺ ☺ ☹	Hot Tub	☺ ☺ ☹
☐ Ice	☐ Security	☐ Quiet	☐ Noisy			

PLACES VISITED / ACTIVITIES: _____

_____
_____
_____

PEOPLE MET / NEW FRIENDS: _____

_____
_____
_____

FOOD, DINING & RESTAURANTS: _____

_____
_____
_____

HIGHLIGHTS / MEMORABLE EVENTS: _____

_____
_____
_____

PLACES TO GO & THINGS TO DO FOR NEXT TIME: _____

_____
_____
_____
_____

NOTES:

Date: _____

Weather:

☀ ⛅ ☔ ❄

🌡 🌡 📢 ☁

From: _____

To: _____

Route Taken: _____

_____

Beginning Mileage:
_____

Ending Mileage:
_____

Total Miles Traveled:
_____

CAMPGROUND INFORMATION

Name: _____

Address: _____

Phone: _____

Site # _____ $ _____ ☐ Day ☐ Week ☐ Month

☐ First Visit
☐ Site Level
☐ 15 amp
☐ Water
☐ Paved
☐ Picnic Table
☐ Patio
☐ Store
☐ Ice

☐ Return Visit
☐ Back-in
☐ 30 amp
☐ Sewer
☐ Sand / Grass
☐ Fire ring
☐ Kid Friendly
☐ Cafe
☐ Security

☐ Easy Access
☐ Pull-through
☐ 50 amp
☐ Shade ☐ Sun
☐ Gravel
☐ Trees ☐ Lawn
☐ Pet Friendly
☐ Firewood
☐ Quiet ☐ Noisy

Our Rating: ☆ ☆ ☆ ☆ ☆

GPS: _____

Altitude: _____

Cell Service / Carrier: _____

☐ Antenna Reception   ☐ Satellite TV   ☐ Cable TV
☐ WIFI Available   ☐ Free ☐ Fee $ _____

Memberships: _____

Amenities: _____

Location	☺	☺	☹	Water Pressure	☺	☺	☹
Restrooms	☺	☺	☹	Laundry	☺	☺	☹
Pool	☺	☺	☹	Hot Tub	☺	☺	☹

PLACES VISITED / ACTIVITIES: _____

_____

_____

_____

PEOPLE MET / NEW FRIENDS: _____

_____

_____

_____

FOOD, DINING & RESTAURANTS: _____

_____

_____

_____

HIGHLIGHTS / MEMORABLE EVENTS: _____

_____

_____

_____

PLACES TO GO & THINGS TO DO FOR NEXT TIME: _____

_____

_____

_____

_____

NOTES:

Date: _____

From: _____

Beginning Mileage: _____

Weather:

To: _____

Ending Mileage: _____

Route Taken: _____

_____

Total Miles Traveled: _____

CAMPGROUND INFORMATION

Name: _____

Our Rating: ☆ ☆ ☆ ☆ ☆

Address: _____

GPS: _____

Phone: _____

Altitude: _____

Site # _____ $ _____ ☐ Day ☐ Week ☐ Month

Cell Service / Carrier: _____

☐ First Visit ☐ Return Visit ☐ Easy Access

☐ Antenna Reception ☐ Satellite TV ☐ Cable TV

☐ Site Level ☐ Back-in ☐ Pull-through

☐ WIFI Available ☐ Free ☐ Fee $ _____

☐ 15 amp ☐ 30 amp ☐ 50 amp

☐ Water ☐ Sewer ☐ Shade ☐ Sun

Memberships: _____

☐ Paved ☐ Sand / Grass ☐ Gravel

Amenities: _____

☐ Picnic Table ☐ Fire ring ☐ Trees ☐ Lawn

Location	☺	☺	☹	Water Pressure	☺ ☺ ☹
Restrooms	☺	☺	☹	Laundry	☺ ☺ ☹
Pool	☺	☺	☹	Hot Tub	☺ ☺ ☹

☐ Patio ☐ Kid Friendly ☐ Pet Friendly

☐ Store ☐ Cafe ☐ Firewood

☐ Ice ☐ Security ☐ Quiet ☐ Noisy

PLACES VISITED / ACTIVITIES: _____

_____

_____

_____

PEOPLE MET / NEW FRIENDS: _____

_____

_____

_____

FOOD, DINING & RESTAURANTS: _____

_____

_____

_____

HIGHLIGHTS / MEMORABLE EVENTS: _____

_____

_____

_____

PLACES TO GO & THINGS TO DO FOR NEXT TIME: _____

_____

_____

_____

_____

NOTES:

Date: _____

Weather:

☀ ☁ ☂ ❄
🌡 🌡 🪁 ☁

From: _____

To: _____

Route Taken: _____
_____

Beginning Mileage: _____

Ending Mileage: _____

Total Miles Traveled: _____

Campground Information

Name: _____

Address: _____

Phone: _____

Site # _____ $ _____ ☐ Day ☐ Week ☐ Month

☐ First Visit
☐ Site Level
☐ 15 amp
☐ Water
☐ Paved
☐ Picnic Table
☐ Patio
☐ Store
☐ Ice

☐ Return Visit
☐ Back-in
☐ 30 amp
☐ Sewer
☐ Sand / Grass
☐ Fire ring
☐ Kid Friendly
☐ Cafe
☐ Security

☐ Easy Access
☐ Pull-through
☐ 50 amp
☐ Shade ☐ Sun
☐ Gravel
☐ Trees ☐ Lawn
☐ Pet Friendly
☐ Firewood
☐ Quiet ☐ Noisy

Our Rating: ☆ ☆ ☆ ☆ ☆

GPS: _____

Altitude: _____

Cell Service / Carrier: _____

☐ Antenna Reception   ☐ Satellite TV   ☐ Cable TV
☐ WIFI Available   ☐ Free ☐ Fee $ _____

Memberships: _____

Amenities: _____

Location	☺	😐	☹	Water Pressure	☺	😐	☹
Restrooms	☺	😐	☹	Laundry	☺	😐	☹
Pool	☺	😐	☹	Hot Tub	☺	😐	☹

Places Visited / Activities: _____
_____
_____
_____

People Met / New Friends: _____
_____
_____
_____

Food, Dining & Restaurants: _____
_____
_____
_____

Highlights / Memorable Events: _____
_____
_____
_____

Places To Go & Things To Do for Next Time: _____
_____
_____
_____
_____

NOTES:

Date: _____	From: _____	Beginning Mileage:
Weather:	To: _____	_____
	Route Taken: _____	Ending Mileage:
	_____	Total Miles Traveled:

CAMPGROUND INFORMATION

Name: _____

Our Rating: ☆ ☆ ☆ ☆ ☆

Address: _____

GPS: _____

Phone: _____

Altitude: _____

Site # _____ $ _____ ☐ Day ☐ Week ☐ Month

Cell Service / Carrier: _____

☐ First Visit	☐ Return Visit	☐ Easy Access
☐ Site Level	☐ Back-in	☐ Pull-through
☐ 15 amp	☐ 30 amp	☐ 50 amp
☐ Water	☐ Sewer	☐ Shade ☐ Sun
☐ Paved	☐ Sand / Grass	☐ Gravel
☐ Picnic Table	☐ Fire ring	☐ Trees ☐ Lawn
☐ Patio	☐ Kid Friendly	☐ Pet Friendly
☐ Store	☐ Cafe	☐ Firewood
☐ Ice	☐ Security	☐ Quiet ☐ Noisy

☐ Antenna Reception   ☐ Satellite TV   ☐ Cable TV

☐ WIFI Available   ☐ Free   ☐ Fee $ _____

Memberships: _____

Amenities: _____

Location	☺ ☺ ☹	Water Pressure	☺ ☺ ☹
Restrooms	☺ ☺ ☹	Laundry	☺ ☺ ☹
Pool	☺ ☺ ☹	Hot Tub	☺ ☺ ☹

PLACES VISITED / ACTIVITIES: _____

_____

_____

_____

PEOPLE MET / NEW FRIENDS: _____

_____

_____

_____

FOOD, DINING & RESTAURANTS: _____

_____

_____

_____

HIGHLIGHTS / MEMORABLE EVENTS: _____

_____

_____

_____

PLACES TO GO & THINGS TO DO FOR NEXT TIME: _____

_____

_____

_____

_____

NOTES:

Date: _____	From: _____	Beginning Mileage:
	To: _____	_____
Weather:	Route Taken: _____	Ending Mileage:
☀ ⛅ ☂ ❄	_____	_____
🌡 🌡 🚩 ☁		Total Miles Traveled:

CAMPGROUND INFORMATION

Name: _____

Address: _____

Phone: _____

Site # _____ $ _____

☐ First Visit	☐ Return Visit	☐ Easy Access
☐ Site Level	☐ Back-in	☐ Pull-through
☐ 15 amp	☐ 30 amp	☐ 50 amp
☐ Water	☐ Sewer	☐ Shade ☐ Sun
☐ Paved	☐ Sand / Grass	☐ Gravel
☐ Picnic Table	☐ Fire ring	☐ Trees ☐ Lawn
☐ Patio	☐ Kid Friendly	☐ Pet Friendly
☐ Store	☐ Cafe	☐ Firewood
☐ Ice	☐ Security	☐ Quiet ☐ Noisy

Our Rating: ☆ ☆ ☆ ☆ ☆

GPS: _____

Altitude: _____

Cell Service / Carrier: _____

☐ Antenna Reception   ☐ Satellite TV   ☐ Cable TV

☐ WIFI Available   ☐ Free ☐ Fee $ _____

Memberships: _____

Amenities: _____

Location	☺	😐	☹	Water Pressure	☺	😐	☹
Restrooms	☺	😐	☹	Laundry	☺	😐	☹
Pool	☺	😐	☹	Hot Tub	☺	😐	☹

PLACES VISITED / ACTIVITIES: _____

_____

_____

_____

_____

PEOPLE MET / NEW FRIENDS: _____

_____

_____

_____

_____

FOOD, DINING & RESTAURANTS: _____

_____

_____

_____

_____

HIGHLIGHTS / MEMORABLE EVENTS: _____

_____

_____

_____

_____

PLACES TO GO & THINGS TO DO FOR NEXT TIME: _____

_____

_____

_____

_____

NOTES:

Date: _____	From: _____	Beginning Mileage:
Weather:	To: _____	_____
	Route Taken: _____	Ending Mileage:
	_____	Total Miles Traveled:

CAMPGROUND INFORMATION

Name: _____

Address: _____

Phone: _____

Site # _____ $ _____ ☐ Day ☐ Week ☐ Month

☐ First Visit   ☐ Return Visit   ☐ Easy Access
☐ Site Level   ☐ Back-in   ☐ Pull-through
☐ 15 amp   ☐ 30 amp   ☐ 50 amp
☐ Water   ☐ Sewer   ☐ Shade   ☐ Sun
☐ Paved   ☐ Sand / Grass   ☐ Gravel
☐ Picnic Table   ☐ Fire ring   ☐ Trees   ☐ Lawn
☐ Patio   ☐ Kid Friendly   ☐ Pet Friendly
☐ Store   ☐ Cafe   ☐ Firewood
☐ Ice   ☐ Security   ☐ Quiet   ☐ Noisy

Our Rating: ☆ ☆ ☆ ☆ ☆

GPS: _____

Altitude: _____

Cell Service / Carrier: _____

☐ Antenna Reception   ☐ Satellite TV   ☐ Cable TV
☐ WIFI Available   ☐ Free ☐ Fee $ _____

Memberships: _____

Amenities: _____

Location	☺ ☺ ☹	Water Pressure	☺ ☺ ☹
Restrooms	☺ ☺ ☹	Laundry	☺ ☺ ☹
Pool	☺ ☺ ☹	Hot Tub	☺ ☺ ☹

PLACES VISITED / ACTIVITIES: _____
_____
_____
_____

PEOPLE MET / NEW FRIENDS: _____
_____
_____
_____

FOOD, DINING & RESTAURANTS: _____
_____
_____
_____

HIGHLIGHTS / MEMORABLE EVENTS: _____
_____
_____
_____

PLACES TO GO & THINGS TO DO FOR NEXT TIME: _____
_____
_____
_____
_____

NOTES:

Date: _____	From: _____	Beginning Mileage: _____
Weather:	To: _____	Ending Mileage: _____
	Route Taken: _____	
	_____	Total Miles Traveled: _____

CAMPGROUND INFORMATION

Name: _____

Our Rating: ☆ ☆ ☆ ☆ ☆

Address: _____

GPS: _____

Phone: _____

Altitude: _____

Site # _____ $ _____

Cell Service / Carrier: _____

- ☐ Day ☐ Week ☐ Month

- ☐ First Visit
- ☐ Site Level
- ☐ 15 amp
- ☐ Water
- ☐ Paved
- ☐ Picnic Table
- ☐ Patio
- ☐ Store
- ☐ Ice

- ☐ Return Visit
- ☐ Back-in
- ☐ 30 amp
- ☐ Sewer
- ☐ Sand / Grass
- ☐ Fire ring
- ☐ Kid Friendly
- ☐ Cafe
- ☐ Security

- ☐ Easy Access
- ☐ Pull-through
- ☐ 50 amp
- ☐ Shade ☐ Sun
- ☐ Gravel
- ☐ Trees ☐ Lawn
- ☐ Pet Friendly
- ☐ Firewood
- ☐ Quiet ☐ Noisy

- ☐ Antenna Reception   ☐ Satellite TV   ☐ Cable TV
- ☐ WIFI Available   ☐ Free ☐ Fee $ _____

Memberships: _____

Amenities: _____

Location	☺	😐	☹	Water Pressure	☺	😐	☹
Restrooms	☺	😐	☹	Laundry	☺	😐	☹
Pool	☺	😐	☹	Hot Tub	☺	😐	☹

PLACES VISITED / ACTIVITIES: _____

_____
_____
_____
_____

PEOPLE MET / NEW FRIENDS: _____

_____
_____
_____
_____

FOOD, DINING & RESTAURANTS: _____

_____
_____
_____
_____

HIGHLIGHTS / MEMORABLE EVENTS: _____

_____
_____
_____
_____

PLACES TO GO & THINGS TO DO FOR NEXT TIME: _____

_____
_____
_____
_____

NOTES:

Date: _____	From: _____	Beginning Mileage: _____
Weather:	To: _____	_____
	Route Taken: _____	Ending Mileage: _____
	_____	Total Miles Traveled: _____

CAMPGROUND INFORMATION

Name: _____

Address: _____

Phone: _____

Our Rating: ☆ ☆ ☆ ☆ ☆

GPS: _____

Altitude: _____

Site # _____ $ _____ ☐ Day ☐ Week ☐ Month

Cell Service / Carrier: _____

☐ First Visit   ☐ Return Visit   ☐ Easy Access
☐ Site Level   ☐ Back-in   ☐ Pull-through
☐ 15 amp   ☐ 30 amp   ☐ 50 amp
☐ Water   ☐ Sewer   ☐ Shade   ☐ Sun
☐ Paved   ☐ Sand / Grass   ☐ Gravel
☐ Picnic Table   ☐ Fire ring   ☐ Trees   ☐ Lawn
☐ Patio   ☐ Kid Friendly   ☐ Pet Friendly
☐ Store   ☐ Cafe   ☐ Firewood
☐ Ice   ☐ Security   ☐ Quiet   ☐ Noisy

☐ Antenna Reception   ☐ Satellite TV   ☐ Cable TV
☐ WIFI Available   ☐ Free ☐ Fee $ _____

Memberships: _____

Amenities: _____

Location	☺ ☺ ☹	Water Pressure	☺ ☺ ☹
Restrooms	☺ ☺ ☹	Laundry	☺ ☺ ☹
Pool	☺ ☺ ☹	Hot Tub	☺ ☺ ☹

PLACES VISITED / ACTIVITIES: _____

_____

_____

_____

PEOPLE MET / NEW FRIENDS: _____

_____

_____

_____

FOOD, DINING & RESTAURANTS: _____

_____

_____

_____

HIGHLIGHTS / MEMORABLE EVENTS: _____

_____

_____

_____

PLACES TO GO & THINGS TO DO FOR NEXT TIME: _____

_____

_____

_____

_____

NOTES:

Date: _____

Weather:

☀ ⛅ ☂ ❄

🌡 🌡 🔦 ☁

From: _____

To: _____

Route Taken: _____

_____

Beginning Mileage: _____

_____

Ending Mileage: _____

_____

Total Miles Traveled: _____

CAMPGROUND INFORMATION

Name: _____

Address: _____

Phone: _____

Site # _____ $ _____ ☐ Day ☐ Week ☐ Month

☐ First Visit   ☐ Return Visit   ☐ Easy Access
☐ Site Level   ☐ Back-in   ☐ Pull-through
☐ 15 amp   ☐ 30 amp   ☐ 50 amp
☐ Water   ☐ Sewer   ☐ Shade   ☐ Sun
☐ Paved   ☐ Sand / Grass   ☐ Gravel
☐ Picnic Table   ☐ Fire ring   ☐ Trees   ☐ Lawn
☐ Patio   ☐ Kid Friendly   ☐ Pet Friendly
☐ Store   ☐ Cafe   ☐ Firewood
☐ Ice   ☐ Security   ☐ Quiet   ☐ Noisy

Our Rating: ☆ ☆ ☆ ☆ ☆

GPS: _____

Altitude: _____

Cell Service / Carrier: _____

☐ Antenna Reception   ☐ Satellite TV   ☐ Cable TV
☐ WIFI Available   ☐ Free ☐ Fee $ _____

Memberships: _____

Amenities: _____

Location   ☺ ☺ ☹   Water Pressure   ☺ ☺ ☹
Restrooms   ☺ ☺ ☹   Laundry   ☺ ☺ ☹
Pool   ☺ ☺ ☹   Hot Tub   ☺ ☺ ☹

PLACES VISITED / ACTIVITIES: _____

_____

_____

_____

PEOPLE MET / NEW FRIENDS: _____

_____

_____

_____

FOOD, DINING & RESTAURANTS: _____

_____

_____

_____

HIGHLIGHTS / MEMORABLE EVENTS: _____

_____

_____

_____

PLACES TO GO & THINGS TO DO FOR NEXT TIME: _____

_____

_____

_____

_____

NOTES:

Date: _____	From: _____	Beginning Mileage:
Weather:	To: _____	_____
	Route Taken: _____	Ending Mileage:
	_____	_____
		Total Miles Traveled:

CAMPGROUND INFORMATION

Name: _____

Address: _____

Phone: _____

Our Rating: ☆ ☆ ☆ ☆ ☆

GPS: _____

Altitude: _____

Site # _____ $ _____ ☐ Day ☐ Week ☐ Month

Cell Service / Carrier: _____

☐ First Visit	☐ Return Visit	☐ Easy Access	
☐ Site Level	☐ Back-in	☐ Pull-through	
☐ 15 amp	☐ 30 amp	☐ 50 amp	
☐ Water	☐ Sewer	☐ Shade	☐ Sun
☐ Paved	☐ Sand / Grass	☐ Gravel	
☐ Picnic Table	☐ Fire ring	☐ Trees	☐ Lawn
☐ Patio	☐ Kid Friendly	☐ Pet Friendly	
☐ Store	☐ Cafe	☐ Firewood	
☐ Ice	☐ Security	☐ Quiet	☐ Noisy

☐ Antenna Reception ☐ Satellite TV ☐ Cable TV
☐ WIFI Available ☐ Free ☐ Fee $ _____

Memberships: _____

Amenities: _____

Location	☺ ☺ ☹	Water Pressure	☺ ☺ ☹
Restrooms	☺ ☺ ☹	Laundry	☺ ☺ ☹
Pool	☺ ☺ ☹	Hot Tub	☺ ☺ ☹

PLACES VISITED / ACTIVITIES: _____
_____
_____
_____

PEOPLE MET / NEW FRIENDS: _____
_____
_____
_____

FOOD, DINING & RESTAURANTS: _____
_____
_____
_____

HIGHLIGHTS / MEMORABLE EVENTS: _____
_____
_____
_____

PLACES TO GO & THINGS TO DO FOR NEXT TIME: _____
_____
_____
_____
_____

NOTES:

Date: _____	From: _____	Beginning Mileage:
	To: _____	_____
Weather:	Route Taken: _____	Ending Mileage:
☀ ☁ ☂ ❄	_____	_____
🌡 🌡 🎏 ☁		Total Miles Traveled:

CAMPGROUND INFORMATION

Name: _____

Address: _____

Phone: _____

Site # _____ $ _____ ☐ Day ☐ Week ☐ Month

☐ First Visit ☐ Return Visit ☐ Easy Access
☐ Site Level ☐ Back-in ☐ Pull-through
☐ 15 amp ☐ 30 amp ☐ 50 amp
☐ Water ☐ Sewer ☐ Shade ☐ Sun
☐ Paved ☐ Sand / Grass ☐ Gravel
☐ Picnic Table ☐ Fire ring ☐ Trees ☐ Lawn
☐ Patio ☐ Kid Friendly ☐ Pet Friendly
☐ Store ☐ Cafe ☐ Firewood
☐ Ice ☐ Security ☐ Quiet ☐ Noisy

Our Rating: ☆ ☆ ☆ ☆ ☆

GPS: _____

Altitude: _____

Cell Service / Carrier: _____

☐ Antenna Reception ☐ Satellite TV ☐ Cable TV
☐ WIFI Available ☐ Free ☐ Fee $ _____

Memberships: _____

Amenities: _____

Location	🙂 😐 🙁	Water Pressure	🙂 😐 🙁
Restrooms	🙂 😐 🙁	Laundry	🙂 😐 🙁
Pool	🙂 😐 🙁	Hot Tub	🙂 😐 🙁

PLACES VISITED / ACTIVITIES: _____
_____
_____
_____

PEOPLE MET / NEW FRIENDS: _____
_____
_____
_____

FOOD, DINING & RESTAURANTS: _____
_____
_____
_____

HIGHLIGHTS / MEMORABLE EVENTS: _____
_____
_____
_____

PLACES TO GO & THINGS TO DO FOR NEXT TIME: _____
_____
_____
_____
_____

NOTES:

Date: _____

Weather:

☀ ☁ ☂ ❄

🌡 🌡 🚩 ☁

From: _____

To: _____

Route Taken: _____

_____

Beginning Mileage: _____

_____

Ending Mileage: _____

_____

Total Miles Traveled: _____

CAMPGROUND INFORMATION

Name: _____

Address: _____

Phone: _____

Our Rating: ☆ ☆ ☆ ☆ ☆

GPS: _____

Altitude: _____

Cell Service / Carrier: _____

Site # _____ $ _____ ☐ Day ☐ Week ☐ Month

☐ First Visit	☐ Return Visit	☐ Easy Access
☐ Site Level	☐ Back-in	☐ Pull-through
☐ 15 amp	☐ 30 amp	☐ 50 amp
☐ Water	☐ Sewer	☐ Shade ☐ Sun
☐ Paved	☐ Sand / Grass	☐ Gravel
☐ Picnic Table	☐ Fire ring	☐ Trees ☐ Lawn
☐ Patio	☐ Kid Friendly	☐ Pet Friendly
☐ Store	☐ Cafe	☐ Firewood
☐ Ice	☐ Security	☐ Quiet ☐ Noisy

☐ Antenna Reception   ☐ Satellite TV   ☐ Cable TV

☐ WIFI Available   ☐ Free   ☐ Fee $ _____

Memberships: _____

Amenities: _____

Location	☺	☺	☹	Water Pressure	☺	☺	☹
Restrooms	☺	☺	☹	Laundry	☺	☺	☹
Pool	☺	☺	☹	Hot Tub	☺	☺	☹

PLACES VISITED / ACTIVITIES: _____

_____

_____

_____

PEOPLE MET / NEW FRIENDS: _____

_____

_____

_____

FOOD, DINING & RESTAURANTS: _____

_____

_____

_____

HIGHLIGHTS / MEMORABLE EVENTS: _____

_____

_____

_____

PLACES TO GO & THINGS TO DO FOR NEXT TIME: _____

_____

_____

_____

_____

NOTES:

Date: _____   From: _____   Beginning Mileage: _____

Weather: To: _____   Ending Mileage: _____

☀ ☁ ☂ ❄   Route Taken: _____
🌡 🌡 🎐 💨   _____   Total Miles Traveled: _____

Campground Information

Name: _____   Our Rating: ☆ ☆ ☆ ☆ ☆

Address: _____   GPS: _____

Phone: _____   Altitude: _____

Site # _____ $ _____ ☐ Day ☐ Week ☐ Month   Cell Service / Carrier: _____

☐ First Visit   ☐ Return Visit   ☐ Easy Access   ☐ Antenna Reception   ☐ Satellite TV   ☐ Cable TV
☐ Site Level   ☐ Back-in   ☐ Pull-through   ☐ WIFI Available   ☐ Free   ☐ Fee $ _____
☐ 15 amp   ☐ 30 amp   ☐ 50 amp
☐ Water   ☐ Sewer   ☐ Shade   ☐ Sun   Memberships: _____
☐ Paved   ☐ Sand / Grass   ☐ Gravel   Amenities: _____
☐ Picnic Table   ☐ Fire ring   ☐ Trees   ☐ Lawn
☐ Patio   ☐ Kid Friendly   ☐ Pet Friendly   Location   ☺ ☺ ☹   Water Pressure   ☺ ☺ ☹
☐ Store   ☐ Cafe   ☐ Firewood   Restrooms ☺ ☺ ☹   Laundry   ☺ ☺ ☹
☐ Ice   ☐ Security   ☐ Quiet   ☐ Noisy Pool   ☺ ☺ ☹   Hot Tub   ☺ ☺ ☹

PLACES VISITED / ACTIVITIES: _____
_____
_____
_____
_____

PEOPLE MET / NEW FRIENDS: _____
_____
_____
_____
_____

FOOD, DINING & RESTAURANTS: _____
_____
_____
_____
_____

HIGHLIGHTS / MEMORABLE EVENTS: _____
_____
_____
_____
_____

PLACES TO GO & THINGS TO DO FOR NEXT TIME: _____
_____
_____
_____
_____

NOTES:

Date: _____	From: _____	Beginning Mileage:
	To: _____	_____
Weather:	Route Taken: _____	Ending Mileage:
☀ ⛅ ☂ ❄	_____	_____
🌡 ❄🌡 🎐 ☁		Total Miles Traveled:

CAMPGROUND INFORMATION

Name: _____	Our Rating: ☆ ☆ ☆ ☆ ☆
Address: _____	GPS: _____
Phone: _____	Altitude: _____

Site # _____ $ _____ ☐ Day ☐ Week ☐ Month

Cell Service / Carrier: _____

☐ First Visit	☐ Return Visit	☐ Easy Access
☐ Site Level	☐ Back-in	☐ Pull-through
☐ 15 amp	☐ 30 amp	☐ 50 amp
☐ Water	☐ Sewer	☐ Shade ☐ Sun
☐ Paved	☐ Sand / Grass	☐ Gravel
☐ Picnic Table	☐ Fire ring	☐ Trees ☐ Lawn
☐ Patio	☐ Kid Friendly	☐ Pet Friendly
☐ Store	☐ Cafe	☐ Firewood
☐ Ice	☐ Security	☐ Quiet ☐ Noisy

☐ Antenna Reception   ☐ Satellite TV   ☐ Cable TV
☐ WIFI Available   ☐ Free   ☐ Fee $ _____

Memberships: _____

Amenities: _____

Location	☺ ☺ ☹	Water Pressure	☺ ☺ ☹
Restrooms	☺ ☺ ☹	Laundry	☺ ☺ ☹
Pool	☺ ☺ ☹	Hot Tub	☺ ☺ ☹

PLACES VISITED / ACTIVITIES: _____
_____
_____
_____

PEOPLE MET / NEW FRIENDS: _____
_____
_____
_____

FOOD, DINING & RESTAURANTS: _____
_____
_____
_____

HIGHLIGHTS / MEMORABLE EVENTS: _____
_____
_____
_____

PLACES TO GO & THINGS TO DO FOR NEXT TIME: _____
_____
_____
_____
_____

NOTES:

Date: _____

Weather:

☀ ☁ ☔ ❄
🌡 🌡 📢 🌩

From: _____

To: _____

Route Taken: _____

_____

Beginning Mileage: _____

Ending Mileage: _____

Total Miles Traveled: _____

Campground Information

Name: _____

Address: _____

Phone: _____

Site # _____ $ _____ ☐ Day ☐ Week ☐ Month

☐ First Visit ☐ Return Visit ☐ Easy Access
☐ Site Level ☐ Back-in ☐ Pull-through
☐ 15 amp ☐ 30 amp ☐ 50 amp
☐ Water ☐ Sewer ☐ Shade ☐ Sun
☐ Paved ☐ Sand / Grass ☐ Gravel
☐ Picnic Table ☐ Fire ring ☐ Trees ☐ Lawn
☐ Patio ☐ Kid Friendly ☐ Pet Friendly
☐ Store ☐ Cafe ☐ Firewood
☐ Ice ☐ Security ☐ Quiet ☐ Noisy

Our Rating: ☆ ☆ ☆ ☆ ☆

GPS: _____

Altitude: _____

Cell Service / Carrier: _____

☐ Antenna Reception ☐ Satellite TV ☐ Cable TV
☐ WIFI Available ☐ Free ☐ Fee $ _____

Memberships: _____

Amenities: _____

Location	☺	☺	☹	Water Pressure	☺	☺	☹
Restrooms	☺	☺	☹	Laundry	☺	☺	☹
Pool	☺	☺	☹	Hot Tub	☺	☺	☹

Places Visited / Activities: _____

_____
_____
_____

People Met / New Friends: _____

_____
_____
_____

Food, Dining & Restaurants: _____

_____
_____
_____

Highlights / Memorable Events: _____

_____
_____
_____

Places To Go & Things To Do for Next Time: _____

_____
_____
_____
_____

NOTES:

Date: _____

Weather:

☀ ⛅ ☔ ❄

🌡 🌡 📢 ☁

From: _____

To: _____

Route Taken: _____

_____

Beginning Mileage: _____

_____

Ending Mileage: _____

_____

Total Miles Traveled: _____

CAMPGROUND INFORMATION

Name: _____

Address: _____

Phone: _____

Site # _____ $ _____ ☐ Day ☐ Week ☐ Month

☐ First Visit   ☐ Return Visit   ☐ Easy Access
☐ Site Level   ☐ Back-in   ☐ Pull-through
☐ 15 amp   ☐ 30 amp   ☐ 50 amp
☐ Water   ☐ Sewer   ☐ Shade   ☐ Sun
☐ Paved   ☐ Sand / Grass   ☐ Gravel
☐ Picnic Table   ☐ Fire ring   ☐ Trees   ☐ Lawn
☐ Patio   ☐ Kid Friendly   ☐ Pet Friendly
☐ Store   ☐ Cafe   ☐ Firewood
☐ Ice   ☐ Security   ☐ Quiet   ☐ Noisy

Our Rating: ☆ ☆ ☆ ☆ ☆

GPS: _____

Altitude: _____

Cell Service / Carrier: _____

☐ Antenna Reception   ☐ Satellite TV   ☐ Cable TV
☐ WIFI Available   ☐ Free ☐ Fee $ _____

Memberships: _____

Amenities: _____

Location	☺	☺	☹	Water Pressure	☺	☺	☹
Restrooms	☺	☺	☹	Laundry	☺	☺	☹
Pool	☺	☺	☹	Hot Tub	☺	☺	☹

PLACES VISITED / ACTIVITIES: _____

_____

_____

_____

_____

PEOPLE MET / NEW FRIENDS: _____

_____

_____

_____

_____

FOOD, DINING & RESTAURANTS: _____

_____

_____

_____

_____

HIGHLIGHTS / MEMORABLE EVENTS: _____

_____

_____

_____

_____

PLACES TO GO & THINGS TO DO FOR NEXT TIME: _____

_____

_____

_____

_____

NOTES:

Date: _____

Weather:

From: _____

To: _____

Route Taken: _____
_____

Beginning Mileage: _____
_____

Ending Mileage: _____
_____

Total Miles Traveled: _____

CAMPGROUND INFORMATION

Name: _____

Address: _____

Phone: _____

Our Rating: ☆ ☆ ☆ ☆ ☆

GPS: _____

Altitude: _____

Site # _____ $ _____ ☐ Day ☐ Week ☐ Month

☐ First Visit
☐ Site Level
☐ 15 amp
☐ Water
☐ Paved
☐ Picnic Table
☐ Patio
☐ Store
☐ Ice

☐ Return Visit
☐ Back-in
☐ 30 amp
☐ Sewer
☐ Sand / Grass
☐ Fire ring
☐ Kid Friendly
☐ Cafe
☐ Security

☐ Easy Access
☐ Pull-through
☐ 50 amp
☐ Shade   ☐ Sun
☐ Gravel
☐ Trees   ☐ Lawn
☐ Pet Friendly
☐ Firewood
☐ Quiet   ☐ Noisy

Cell Service / Carrier: _____

☐ Antenna Reception   ☐ Satellite TV   ☐ Cable TV
☐ WIFI Available   ☐ Free ☐ Fee $ _____

Memberships: _____

Amenities: _____

Location	☺	☺	☹	Water Pressure	☺	☺	☹
Restrooms	☺	☺	☹	Laundry	☺	☺	☹
Pool	☺	☺	☹	Hot Tub	☺	☺	☹

PLACES VISITED / ACTIVITIES: _____
_____
_____
_____

PEOPLE MET / NEW FRIENDS: _____
_____
_____
_____

FOOD, DINING & RESTAURANTS: _____
_____
_____
_____

HIGHLIGHTS / MEMORABLE EVENTS: _____
_____
_____
_____

PLACES TO GO & THINGS TO DO FOR NEXT TIME: _____
_____
_____
_____
_____

NOTES:

Date: _____	From: _____	Beginning Mileage:
	To: _____	_____
Weather:		Ending Mileage:
☀ ⛅ ☂ ❄	Route Taken: _____	_____
🌡 ❄🌡 🚩 🌫	_____	Total Miles Traveled:

Campground Information

	Our Rating: ☆ ☆ ☆ ☆ ☆
Name: _____	GPS: _____
Address: _____	Altitude: _____
Phone: _____	Cell Service / Carrier: _____

Site # _____ $ _____ ☐ Day ☐ Week ☐ Month

☐ First Visit ☐ Return Visit ☐ Easy Access
☐ Site Level ☐ Back-in ☐ Pull-through
☐ 15 amp ☐ 30 amp ☐ 50 amp
☐ Water ☐ Sewer ☐ Shade ☐ Sun
☐ Paved ☐ Sand / Grass ☐ Gravel
☐ Picnic Table ☐ Fire ring ☐ Trees ☐ Lawn
☐ Patio ☐ Kid Friendly ☐ Pet Friendly
☐ Store ☐ Cafe ☐ Firewood
☐ Ice ☐ Security ☐ Quiet ☐ Noisy

☐ Antenna Reception ☐ Satellite TV ☐ Cable TV
☐ WIFI Available ☐ Free ☐ Fee $ _____

Memberships: _____

Amenities: _____

Location	☺ ☺ ☹	Water Pressure	☺ ☺ ☹
Restrooms	☺ ☺ ☹	Laundry	☺ ☺ ☹
Pool	☺ ☺ ☹	Hot Tub	☺ ☺ ☹

PLACES VISITED / ACTIVITIES: _____
_____
_____
_____

PEOPLE MET / NEW FRIENDS: _____
_____
_____
_____

FOOD, DINING & RESTAURANTS: _____
_____
_____
_____

HIGHLIGHTS / MEMORABLE EVENTS: _____
_____
_____
_____

PLACES TO GO & THINGS TO DO FOR NEXT TIME: _____
_____
_____
_____
_____

NOTES:

Date: _____	From: _____	Beginning Mileage: _____
Weather:	To: _____	Ending Mileage: _____
☀ ⛅ ☂ ❄ 🌡 🌡 🔦 ☁	Route Taken: _____ _____	Total Miles Traveled: _____

Campground Information

Name: _____	Our Rating: ☆ ☆ ☆ ☆ ☆
Address: _____	GPS: _____
Phone: _____	Altitude: _____

Site # _____ $ _____ ☐ Day ☐ Week ☐ Month

Cell Service / Carrier: _____

☐ First Visit	☐ Return Visit	☐ Easy Access
☐ Site Level	☐ Back-in	☐ Pull-through
☐ 15 amp	☐ 30 amp	☐ 50 amp
☐ Water	☐ Sewer	☐ Shade ☐ Sun
☐ Paved	☐ Sand / Grass	☐ Gravel
☐ Picnic Table	☐ Fire ring	☐ Trees ☐ Lawn
☐ Patio	☐ Kid Friendly	☐ Pet Friendly
☐ Store	☐ Cafe	☐ Firewood
☐ Ice	☐ Security	☐ Quiet ☐ Noisy

☐ Antenna Reception ☐ Satellite TV ☐ Cable TV
☐ WIFI Available ☐ Free ☐ Fee $ _____

Memberships: _____

Amenities: _____

Location	☺ ☺ ☹	Water Pressure	☺ ☺ ☹
Restrooms	☺ ☺ ☹	Laundry	☺ ☺ ☹
Pool	☺ ☺ ☹	Hot Tub	☺ ☺ ☹

Places Visited / Activities: _____
_____
_____
_____

People Met / New Friends: _____
_____
_____
_____

Food, Dining & Restaurants: _____
_____
_____
_____

Highlights / Memorable Events: _____
_____
_____
_____

Places To Go & Things To Do for Next Time: _____
_____
_____
_____
_____

NOTES:

Date:	From:	Beginning Mileage:

Weather:

To:

Route Taken:

Ending Mileage:

Total Miles Traveled:

CAMPGROUND INFORMATION

Name: _____

Address: _____

Phone: _____

Our Rating: ☆ ☆ ☆ ☆ ☆

GPS: _____

Altitude: _____

Site # _____ $ _____ ☐ Day ☐ Week ☐ Month

Cell Service / Carrier: _____

☐ First Visit ☐ Return Visit ☐ Easy Access
☐ Site Level ☐ Back-in ☐ Pull-through
☐ 15 amp ☐ 30 amp ☐ 50 amp
☐ Water ☐ Sewer ☐ Shade ☐ Sun
☐ Paved ☐ Sand / Grass ☐ Gravel
☐ Picnic Table ☐ Fire ring ☐ Trees ☐ Lawn
☐ Patio ☐ Kid Friendly ☐ Pet Friendly
☐ Store ☐ Cafe ☐ Firewood
☐ Ice ☐ Security ☐ Quiet ☐ Noisy

☐ Antenna Reception ☐ Satellite TV ☐ Cable TV
☐ WIFI Available ☐ Free ☐ Fee $ _____

Memberships: _____

Amenities: _____

Location	☺	☺	☹	Water Pressure	☺	☺	☹
Restrooms	☺	☺	☹	Laundry	☺	☺	☹
Pool	☺	☺	☹	Hot Tub	☺	☺	☹

PLACES VISITED / ACTIVITIES: _____

_____

_____

_____

PEOPLE MET / NEW FRIENDS: _____

_____

_____

_____

FOOD, DINING & RESTAURANTS: _____

_____

_____

_____

HIGHLIGHTS / MEMORABLE EVENTS: _____

_____

_____

_____

PLACES TO GO & THINGS TO DO FOR NEXT TIME: _____

_____

_____

_____

_____

NOTES:

Date: _____

Weather:

From: _____

To: _____

Route Taken: _____

_____

Beginning Mileage: _____

Ending Mileage: _____

Total Miles Traveled: _____

CAMPGROUND INFORMATION

Name: _____

Address: _____

Phone: _____

Site # _____ $ _____ ☐ Day ☐ Week ☐ Month

☐ First Visit
☐ Site Level
☐ 15 amp
☐ Water
☐ Paved
☐ Picnic Table
☐ Patio
☐ Store
☐ Ice

☐ Return Visit
☐ Back-in
☐ 30 amp
☐ Sewer
☐ Sand / Grass
☐ Fire ring
☐ Kid Friendly
☐ Cafe
☐ Security

☐ Easy Access
☐ Pull-through
☐ 50 amp
☐ Shade ☐ Sun
☐ Gravel
☐ Trees ☐ Lawn
☐ Pet Friendly
☐ Firewood
☐ Quiet ☐ Noisy

Our Rating: ☆ ☆ ☆ ☆ ☆

GPS: _____

Altitude: _____

Cell Service / Carrier: _____

☐ Antenna Reception   ☐ Satellite TV   ☐ Cable TV
☐ WIFI Available   ☐ Free ☐ Fee $ _____

Memberships: _____

Amenities: _____

Location	☺	😐	☹	Water Pressure	☺	😐	☹
Restrooms	☺	😐	☹	Laundry	☺	😐	☹
Pool	☺	😐	☹	Hot Tub	☺	😐	☹

PLACES VISITED / ACTIVITIES: _____

_____

_____

_____

PEOPLE MET / NEW FRIENDS: _____

_____

_____

_____

FOOD, DINING & RESTAURANTS: _____

_____

_____

_____

HIGHLIGHTS / MEMORABLE EVENTS: _____

_____

_____

_____

PLACES TO GO & THINGS TO DO FOR NEXT TIME: _____

_____

_____

_____

_____

NOTES:

Date: _____

Weather:

From: _____

To: _____

Route Taken: _____

_____

Beginning Mileage: _____

Ending Mileage: _____

Total Miles Traveled: _____

CAMPGROUND INFORMATION

Name: _____

Address: _____

Phone: _____

Site # _____ $ _____ ☐ Day ☐ Week ☐ Month

☐ First Visit ☐ Return Visit ☐ Easy Access
☐ Site Level ☐ Back-in ☐ Pull-through
☐ 15 amp ☐ 30 amp ☐ 50 amp
☐ Water ☐ Sewer ☐ Shade ☐ Sun
☐ Paved ☐ Sand / Grass ☐ Gravel
☐ Picnic Table ☐ Fire ring ☐ Trees ☐ Lawn
☐ Patio ☐ Kid Friendly ☐ Pet Friendly
☐ Store ☐ Cafe ☐ Firewood
☐ Ice ☐ Security ☐ Quiet ☐ Noisy

Our Rating: ☆ ☆ ☆ ☆ ☆

GPS: _____

Altitude: _____

Cell Service / Carrier: _____

☐ Antenna Reception ☐ Satellite TV ☐ Cable TV
☐ WIFI Available ☐ Free ☐ Fee $ _____

Memberships: _____

Amenities: _____

Location	☺	☻	☹	Water Pressure	☺	☻	☹
Restrooms	☺	☻	☹	Laundry	☺	☻	☹
Pool	☺	☻	☹	Hot Tub	☺	☻	☹

PLACES VISITED / ACTIVITIES: _____

_____

_____

_____

PEOPLE MET / NEW FRIENDS: _____

_____

_____

_____

FOOD, DINING & RESTAURANTS: _____

_____

_____

_____

HIGHLIGHTS / MEMORABLE EVENTS: _____

_____

_____

_____

PLACES TO GO & THINGS TO DO FOR NEXT TIME: _____

_____

_____

_____

_____

NOTES:

Date: _____

Weather:

From: _____

To: _____

Route Taken: _____

_____

Beginning Mileage:

_____

Ending Mileage:

_____

Total Miles Traveled:

_____

CAMPGROUND INFORMATION

Name: _____

Address: _____

Phone: _____

Site # _____ $ _____ ☐ Day ☐ Week ☐ Month

☐ First Visit ☐ Return Visit ☐ Easy Access
☐ Site Level ☐ Back-in ☐ Pull-through
☐ 15 amp ☐ 30 amp ☐ 50 amp
☐ Water ☐ Sewer ☐ Shade ☐ Sun
☐ Paved ☐ Sand / Grass ☐ Gravel
☐ Picnic Table ☐ Fire ring ☐ Trees ☐ Lawn
☐ Patio ☐ Kid Friendly ☐ Pet Friendly
☐ Store ☐ Cafe ☐ Firewood
☐ Ice ☐ Security ☐ Quiet ☐ Noisy

Our Rating: ☆ ☆ ☆ ☆ ☆

GPS: _____

Altitude: _____

Cell Service / Carrier: _____

☐ Antenna Reception ☐ Satellite TV ☐ Cable TV
☐ WIFI Available ☐ Free ☐ Fee $ _____

Memberships: _____

Amenities: _____

Location ☺ ☺ ☹   Water Pressure ☺ ☺ ☹
Restrooms ☺ ☺ ☹   Laundry ☺ ☺ ☹
Pool ☺ ☺ ☹   Hot Tub ☺ ☺ ☹

PLACES VISITED / ACTIVITIES: _____

_____

_____

_____

PEOPLE MET / NEW FRIENDS: _____

_____

_____

_____

FOOD, DINING & RESTAURANTS: _____

_____

_____

_____

HIGHLIGHTS / MEMORABLE EVENTS: _____

_____

_____

_____

PLACES TO GO & THINGS TO DO FOR NEXT TIME: _____

_____

_____

_____

_____

NOTES:

Date: _____

Weather:

☀ ⛅ ☔ ❄

🌡 ❄🌡 🚩 ☁

From: _____

To: _____

Route Taken: _____

_____

Beginning Mileage: _____

Ending Mileage: _____

Total Miles Traveled: _____

Campground Information

Name: _____

Address: _____

Phone: _____

Site # _____ $ _____ ☐ Day ☐ Week ☐ Month

☐ First Visit   ☐ Return Visit   ☐ Easy Access
☐ Site Level   ☐ Back-in   ☐ Pull-through
☐ 15 amp   ☐ 30 amp   ☐ 50 amp
☐ Water   ☐ Sewer   ☐ Shade   ☐ Sun
☐ Paved   ☐ Sand / Grass   ☐ Gravel
☐ Picnic Table   ☐ Fire ring   ☐ Trees   ☐ Lawn
☐ Patio   ☐ Kid Friendly   ☐ Pet Friendly
☐ Store   ☐ Cafe   ☐ Firewood
☐ Ice   ☐ Security   ☐ Quiet   ☐ Noisy

Our Rating: ☆ ☆ ☆ ☆ ☆

GPS: _____

Altitude: _____

Cell Service / Carrier: _____

☐ Antenna Reception   ☐ Satellite TV   ☐ Cable TV
☐ WIFI Available   ☐ Free   ☐ Fee $ _____

Memberships: _____

Amenities: _____

Location	☺	☺	☹	Water Pressure	☺	☺	☹
Restrooms	☺	☺	☹	Laundry	☺	☺	☹
Pool	☺	☺	☹	Hot Tub	☺	☺	☹

Places Visited / Activities: _____

_____
_____
_____
_____

People Met / New Friends: _____

_____
_____
_____
_____

Food, Dining & Restaurants: _____

_____
_____
_____

Highlights / Memorable Events: _____

_____
_____
_____

Places To Go & Things To Do for Next Time: _____

_____
_____
_____
_____

NOTES:

Date: _____

Weather:

☀ ⛅ ☂ ❄
🌡 ❄🌡 🚩 ☁

From: _____

To: _____

Route Taken: _____

_____

Beginning Mileage: _____

Ending Mileage: _____

Total Miles Traveled: _____

CAMPGROUND INFORMATION

Name: _____

Address: _____

Phone: _____

Our Rating: ☆ ☆ ☆ ☆ ☆

GPS: _____

Altitude: _____

Site # _____ $ _____ ☐ Day ☐ Week ☐ Month

☐ First Visit   ☐ Return Visit   ☐ Easy Access
☐ Site Level   ☐ Back-in   ☐ Pull-through
☐ 15 amp   ☐ 30 amp   ☐ 50 amp
☐ Water   ☐ Sewer   ☐ Shade   ☐ Sun
☐ Paved   ☐ Sand / Grass   ☐ Gravel
☐ Picnic Table   ☐ Fire ring   ☐ Trees   ☐ Lawn
☐ Patio   ☐ Kid Friendly   ☐ Pet Friendly
☐ Store   ☐ Cafe   ☐ Firewood
☐ Ice   ☐ Security   ☐ Quiet   ☐ Noisy

Cell Service / Carrier: _____

☐ Antenna Reception   ☐ Satellite TV   ☐ Cable TV
☐ WIFI Available   ☐ Free ☐ Fee $ _____

Memberships: _____

Amenities: _____

	☺ ☐ ☹		☺ ☐ ☹
Location	☺ ☐ ☹	Water Pressure	☺ ☐ ☹
Restrooms	☺ ☐ ☹	Laundry	☺ ☐ ☹
Pool	☺ ☐ ☹	Hot Tub	☺ ☐ ☹

PLACES VISITED / ACTIVITIES: _____

_____
_____
_____
_____

PEOPLE MET / NEW FRIENDS: _____

_____
_____
_____
_____

FOOD, DINING & RESTAURANTS: _____

_____
_____
_____
_____

HIGHLIGHTS / MEMORABLE EVENTS: _____

_____
_____
_____
_____

PLACES TO GO & THINGS TO DO FOR NEXT TIME: _____

_____
_____
_____
_____

NOTES:

Date: _____	From: _____	Beginning Mileage: _____
Weather:	To: _____	Ending Mileage: _____
	Route Taken: _____	Total Miles Traveled: _____

Campground Information

Name: _____	Our Rating: ☆ ☆ ☆ ☆ ☆
Address: _____	GPS: _____
Phone: _____	Altitude: _____

Site # _____ $ _____ ☐ Day ☐ Week ☐ Month

Cell Service / Carrier: _____

☐ First Visit	☐ Return Visit	☐ Easy Access
☐ Site Level	☐ Back-in	☐ Pull-through
☐ 15 amp	☐ 30 amp	☐ 50 amp
☐ Water	☐ Sewer	☐ Shade ☐ Sun
☐ Paved	☐ Sand / Grass	☐ Gravel
☐ Picnic Table	☐ Fire ring	☐ Trees ☐ Lawn
☐ Patio	☐ Kid Friendly	☐ Pet Friendly
☐ Store	☐ Cafe	☐ Firewood
☐ Ice	☐ Security	☐ Quiet ☐ Noisy

☐ Antenna Reception ☐ Satellite TV ☐ Cable TV
☐ WIFI Available ☐ Free ☐ Fee $ _____

Memberships: _____

Amenities: _____

Location	☺ ☺ ☹	Water Pressure	☺ ☺ ☹
Restrooms	☺ ☺ ☹	Laundry	☺ ☺ ☹
Pool	☺ ☺ ☹	Hot Tub	☺ ☺ ☹

Places Visited / Activities: _____

_____
_____
_____

People Met / New Friends: _____

_____
_____
_____

Food, Dining & Restaurants: _____

_____
_____
_____

Highlights / Memorable Events: _____

_____
_____
_____

Places To Go & Things To Do for Next Time: _____

_____
_____
_____
_____

NOTES:

Date: _____

Weather:

☀ ⛅ ☂ ❄
🌡 ❄🌡 📢 ☁

From: _____

To: _____

Route Taken: _____

_____

Beginning Mileage: _____

_____

Ending Mileage: _____

_____

Total Miles Traveled: _____

CAMPGROUND INFORMATION

Name: _____

Address: _____

Phone: _____

Site # _____ $ _____

☐ First Visit
☐ Site Level
☐ 15 amp
☐ Water
☐ Paved
☐ Picnic Table
☐ Patio
☐ Store
☐ Ice

☐ Return Visit
☐ Back-in
☐ 30 amp
☐ Sewer
☐ Sand / Grass
☐ Fire ring
☐ Kid Friendly
☐ Cafe
☐ Security

☐ Day ☐ Week ☐ Month
☐ Easy Access
☐ Pull-through
☐ 50 amp
☐ Shade ☐ Sun
☐ Gravel
☐ Trees ☐ Lawn
☐ Pet Friendly
☐ Firewood
☐ Quiet ☐ Noisy

Our Rating: ☆ ☆ ☆ ☆ ☆

GPS: _____

Altitude: _____

Cell Service / Carrier: _____

☐ Antenna Reception   ☐ Satellite TV   ☐ Cable TV
☐ WIFI Available   ☐ Free ☐ Fee $ _____

Memberships: _____

Amenities: _____

Location	☺	☹	☹	Water Pressure	☺	☹	☹
Restrooms	☺	☹	☹	Laundry	☺	☹	☹
Pool	☺	☹	☹	Hot Tub	☺	☹	☹

PLACES VISITED / ACTIVITIES: _____

_____

_____

_____

_____

PEOPLE MET / NEW FRIENDS: _____

_____

_____

_____

FOOD, DINING & RESTAURANTS: _____

_____

_____

_____

HIGHLIGHTS / MEMORABLE EVENTS: _____

_____

_____

_____

_____

PLACES TO GO & THINGS TO DO FOR NEXT TIME: _____

_____

_____

_____

_____

NOTES:

Date: _____

Weather:

☀ ⛅ ☔ ❄
🌡 🌡 🚩 ☁

From: _____

To: _____

Route Taken: _____

_____

Beginning Mileage: _____

_____

Ending Mileage: _____

_____

Total Miles Traveled: _____

CAMPGROUND INFORMATION

Name: _____

Address: _____

Phone: _____

Site # _____ $ _____ ☐ Day ☐ Week ☐ Month

☐ First Visit   ☐ Return Visit   ☐ Easy Access
☐ Site Level   ☐ Back-in   ☐ Pull-through
☐ 15 amp   ☐ 30 amp   ☐ 50 amp
☐ Water   ☐ Sewer   ☐ Shade   ☐ Sun
☐ Paved   ☐ Sand / Grass   ☐ Gravel
☐ Picnic Table   ☐ Fire ring   ☐ Trees   ☐ Lawn
☐ Patio   ☐ Kid Friendly   ☐ Pet Friendly
☐ Store   ☐ Cafe   ☐ Firewood
☐ Ice   ☐ Security   ☐ Quiet   ☐ Noisy

Our Rating: ☆ ☆ ☆ ☆ ☆

GPS: _____

Altitude: _____

Cell Service / Carrier: _____

☐ Antenna Reception   ☐ Satellite TV   ☐ Cable TV
☐ WIFI Available   ☐ Free ☐ Fee $ _____

Memberships: _____

Amenities: _____

Location	☺	☺	☹	Water Pressure	☺	☺	☹
Restrooms	☺	☺	☹	Laundry	☺	☺	☹
Pool	☺	☺	☹	Hot Tub	☺	☺	☹

PLACES VISITED / ACTIVITIES: _____

_____
_____
_____

PEOPLE MET / NEW FRIENDS: _____

_____
_____
_____

FOOD, DINING & RESTAURANTS: _____

_____
_____
_____

HIGHLIGHTS / MEMORABLE EVENTS: _____

_____
_____
_____

PLACES TO GO & THINGS TO DO FOR NEXT TIME: _____

_____
_____
_____
_____

NOTES:

Date: _____	From: _____	Beginning Mileage: _____
Weather:	To: _____	Ending Mileage: _____
	Route Taken: _____	
	_____	Total Miles Traveled: _____

CAMPGROUND INFORMATION

Name: _____

Address: _____

Phone: _____

Site # _____ $ _____ ☐ Day ☐ Week ☐ Month

☐ First Visit ☐ Return Visit ☐ Easy Access
☐ Site Level ☐ Back-in ☐ Pull-through
☐ 15 amp ☐ 30 amp ☐ 50 amp
☐ Water ☐ Sewer ☐ Shade ☐ Sun
☐ Paved ☐ Sand / Grass ☐ Gravel
☐ Picnic Table ☐ Fire ring ☐ Trees ☐ Lawn
☐ Patio ☐ Kid Friendly ☐ Pet Friendly
☐ Store ☐ Cafe ☐ Firewood
☐ Ice ☐ Security ☐ Quiet ☐ Noisy

Our Rating: ☆ ☆ ☆ ☆ ☆

GPS: _____

Altitude: _____

Cell Service / Carrier: _____

☐ Antenna Reception ☐ Satellite TV ☐ Cable TV
☐ WIFI Available ☐ Free ☐ Fee $ _____

Memberships: _____

Amenities: _____

Location	☺	😐	☹	Water Pressure	☺	😐	☹
Restrooms	☺	😐	☹	Laundry	☺	😐	☹
Pool	☺	😐	☹	Hot Tub	☺	😐	☹

PLACES VISITED / ACTIVITIES: _____

_____

_____

_____

PEOPLE MET / NEW FRIENDS: _____

_____

_____

_____

FOOD, DINING & RESTAURANTS: _____

_____

_____

_____

HIGHLIGHTS / MEMORABLE EVENTS: _____

_____

_____

_____

PLACES TO GO & THINGS TO DO FOR NEXT TIME: _____

_____

_____

_____

_____

NOTES:

Date: _____	From: _____	Beginning Mileage:
Weather:	To: _____	_____
	Route Taken: _____	Ending Mileage:
	_____	_____
		Total Miles Traveled:

CAMPGROUND INFORMATION

Name: _____

Our Rating: ☆ ☆ ☆ ☆ ☆

Address: _____

GPS: _____

Phone: _____

Altitude: _____

Site # _____ $ _____ ☐ Day ☐ Week ☐ Month

Cell Service / Carrier: _____

☐ First Visit ☐ Return Visit ☐ Easy Access
☐ Site Level ☐ Back-in ☐ Pull-through
☐ 15 amp ☐ 30 amp ☐ 50 amp
☐ Water ☐ Sewer ☐ Shade ☐ Sun
☐ Paved ☐ Sand / Grass ☐ Gravel
☐ Picnic Table ☐ Fire ring ☐ Trees ☐ Lawn
☐ Patio ☐ Kid Friendly ☐ Pet Friendly
☐ Store ☐ Cafe ☐ Firewood
☐ Ice ☐ Security ☐ Quiet ☐ Noisy

☐ Antenna Reception ☐ Satellite TV ☐ Cable TV
☐ WIFI Available ☐ Free ☐ Fee $ _____

Memberships: _____

Amenities: _____

Location	☺	☺	☹	Water Pressure	☺	☺	☹
Restrooms	☺	☺	☹	Laundry	☺	☺	☹
Pool	☺	☺	☹	Hot Tub	☺	☺	☹

PLACES VISITED / ACTIVITIES: _____

_____

_____

_____

PEOPLE MET / NEW FRIENDS: _____

_____

_____

_____

FOOD, DINING & RESTAURANTS: _____

_____

_____

_____

HIGHLIGHTS / MEMORABLE EVENTS: _____

_____

_____

_____

PLACES TO GO & THINGS TO DO FOR NEXT TIME: _____

_____

_____

_____

_____

NOTES:

Date: _____

Weather:

From: _____

To: _____

Route Taken: _____

_____

Beginning Mileage: _____

Ending Mileage: _____

Total Miles Traveled: _____

CAMPGROUND INFORMATION

Name: _____

Address: _____

Phone: _____

Site # _____ $ _____ ☐ Day ☐ Week ☐ Month

☐ First Visit   ☐ Return Visit   ☐ Easy Access
☐ Site Level   ☐ Back-in   ☐ Pull-through
☐ 15 amp   ☐ 30 amp   ☐ 50 amp
☐ Water   ☐ Sewer   ☐ Shade   ☐ Sun
☐ Paved   ☐ Sand / Grass   ☐ Gravel
☐ Picnic Table   ☐ Fire ring   ☐ Trees   ☐ Lawn
☐ Patio   ☐ Kid Friendly   ☐ Pet Friendly
☐ Store   ☐ Cafe   ☐ Firewood
☐ Ice   ☐ Security   ☐ Quiet   ☐ Noisy

Our Rating: ☆ ☆ ☆ ☆ ☆

GPS: _____

Altitude: _____

Cell Service / Carrier: _____

☐ Antenna Reception   ☐ Satellite TV   ☐ Cable TV
☐ WIFI Available   ☐ Free ☐ Fee $ _____

Memberships: _____

Amenities: _____

Location	☺ ☺ ☹	Water Pressure	☺ ☺ ☹
Restrooms	☺ ☺ ☹	Laundry	☺ ☺ ☹
Pool	☺ ☺ ☹	Hot Tub	☺ ☺ ☹

PLACES VISITED / ACTIVITIES: _____

_____
_____
_____
_____

PEOPLE MET / NEW FRIENDS: _____

_____
_____
_____
_____

FOOD, DINING & RESTAURANTS: _____

_____
_____
_____
_____

HIGHLIGHTS / MEMORABLE EVENTS: _____

_____
_____
_____
_____

PLACES TO GO & THINGS TO DO FOR NEXT TIME: _____

_____
_____
_____
_____
_____

NOTES:

Date: _____	From: _____	Beginning Mileage: _____
	To: _____	
Weather:		Ending Mileage: _____
☀ ⛅ ☂ ❄	Route Taken: _____	
🌡 🌡 🏳 ☁	_____	Total Miles Traveled: _____

CAMPGROUND INFORMATION

Name: _____

Address: _____

Phone: _____

Site # _____ $ _____ ☐ Day ☐ Week ☐ Month

☐ First Visit ☐ Return Visit ☐ Easy Access
☐ Site Level ☐ Back-in ☐ Pull-through
☐ 15 amp ☐ 30 amp ☐ 50 amp
☐ Water ☐ Sewer ☐ Shade ☐ Sun
☐ Paved ☐ Sand / Grass ☐ Gravel
☐ Picnic Table ☐ Fire ring ☐ Trees ☐ Lawn
☐ Patio ☐ Kid Friendly ☐ Pet Friendly
☐ Store ☐ Cafe ☐ Firewood
☐ Ice ☐ Security ☐ Quiet ☐ Noisy

Our Rating: ☆ ☆ ☆ ☆ ☆

GPS: _____

Altitude: _____

Cell Service / Carrier: _____

☐ Antenna Reception ☐ Satellite TV ☐ Cable TV
☐ WIFI Available ☐ Free ☐ Fee $ _____

Memberships: _____

Amenities: _____

Location	☺ ☻ ☹	Water Pressure	☺ ☻ ☹
Restrooms	☺ ☻ ☹	Laundry	☺ ☻ ☹
Pool	☺ ☻ ☹	Hot Tub	☺ ☻ ☹

PLACES VISITED / ACTIVITIES: _____

_____
_____
_____

PEOPLE MET / NEW FRIENDS: _____

_____
_____
_____

FOOD, DINING & RESTAURANTS: _____

_____
_____
_____

HIGHLIGHTS / MEMORABLE EVENTS: _____

_____
_____
_____

PLACES TO GO & THINGS TO DO FOR NEXT TIME: _____

_____
_____
_____
_____

NOTES:

Date: _____	From: _____	Beginning Mileage:
Weather:	To: _____	_____
	Route Taken: _____	Ending Mileage:
	_____	_____
		Total Miles Traveled:

Campground Information

Name: _____

Address: _____

Phone: _____

Our Rating: ☆ ☆ ☆ ☆ ☆

GPS: _____

Altitude: _____

Site # _____ $ _____

Cell Service / Carrier: _____

☐ Day ☐ Week ☐ Month

☐ First Visit   ☐ Return Visit   ☐ Easy Access
☐ Site Level   ☐ Back-in   ☐ Pull-through
☐ 15 amp   ☐ 30 amp   ☐ 50 amp
☐ Water   ☐ Sewer   ☐ Shade   ☐ Sun
☐ Paved   ☐ Sand / Grass   ☐ Gravel
☐ Picnic Table   ☐ Fire ring   ☐ Trees   ☐ Lawn
☐ Patio   ☐ Kid Friendly   ☐ Pet Friendly
☐ Store   ☐ Cafe   ☐ Firewood
☐ Ice   ☐ Security   ☐ Quiet   ☐ Noisy

☐ Antenna Reception   ☐ Satellite TV   ☐ Cable TV
☐ WIFI Available   ☐ Free ☐ Fee $ _____

Memberships: _____

Amenities: _____

Location	☺	☺	☹	Water Pressure	☺	☺	☹
Restrooms	☺	☺	☹	Laundry	☺	☺	☹
Pool	☺	☺	☹	Hot Tub	☺	☺	☹

Places Visited / Activities: _____

_____
_____
_____

People Met / New Friends: _____

_____
_____
_____

Food, Dining & Restaurants: _____

_____
_____
_____
_____

Highlights / Memorable Events: _____

_____
_____
_____

Places To Go & Things To Do for Next Time: _____

_____
_____
_____
_____

NOTES:

Date: _____

Weather:

☀ ☁ ☂ ❄

🌡 🌡 🎐 ☁

From: _____

To: _____

Route Taken: _____

_____

Beginning Mileage: _____

Ending Mileage: _____

Total Miles Traveled: _____

CAMPGROUND INFORMATION

Name: _____

Address: _____

Phone: _____

Site # _____ $ _____

☐ Day ☐ Week ☐ Month

☐ First Visit   ☐ Return Visit   ☐ Easy Access
☐ Site Level   ☐ Back-in   ☐ Pull-through
☐ 15 amp   ☐ 30 amp   ☐ 50 amp
☐ Water   ☐ Sewer   ☐ Shade   ☐ Sun
☐ Paved   ☐ Sand / Grass   ☐ Gravel
☐ Picnic Table   ☐ Fire ring   ☐ Trees   ☐ Lawn
☐ Patio   ☐ Kid Friendly   ☐ Pet Friendly
☐ Store   ☐ Cafe   ☐ Firewood
☐ Ice   ☐ Security   ☐ Quiet   ☐ Noisy

Our Rating: ☆ ☆ ☆ ☆ ☆

GPS: _____

Altitude: _____

Cell Service / Carrier: _____

☐ Antenna Reception   ☐ Satellite TV   ☐ Cable TV
☐ WIFI Available   ☐ Free ☐ Fee $ _____

Memberships: _____

Amenities: _____

Location	☺	☺	☹	Water Pressure	☺	☺	☹
Restrooms	☺	☺	☹	Laundry	☺	☺	☹
Pool	☺	☺	☹	Hot Tub	☺	☺	☹

PLACES VISITED / ACTIVITIES: _____

_____
_____
_____

PEOPLE MET / NEW FRIENDS: _____

_____
_____
_____

FOOD, DINING & RESTAURANTS: _____

_____
_____
_____

HIGHLIGHTS / MEMORABLE EVENTS: _____

_____
_____
_____

PLACES TO GO & THINGS TO DO FOR NEXT TIME: _____

_____
_____
_____
_____

NOTES:

Date:	From:	Beginning Mileage:

Weather:

To:

Route Taken:

Ending Mileage:

Total Miles Traveled:

CAMPGROUND INFORMATION

Name:

Address:

Phone:

Our Rating: ☆ ☆ ☆ ☆ ☆

GPS:

Altitude:

Site # _____ $ _____ ☐ Day ☐ Week ☐ Month

Cell Service / Carrier:

☐ First Visit   ☐ Return Visit   ☐ Easy Access
☐ Site Level   ☐ Back-in   ☐ Pull-through
☐ 15 amp   ☐ 30 amp   ☐ 50 amp
☐ Water   ☐ Sewer   ☐ Shade   ☐ Sun
☐ Paved   ☐ Sand / Grass   ☐ Gravel
☐ Picnic Table   ☐ Fire ring   ☐ Trees   ☐ Lawn
☐ Patio   ☐ Kid Friendly   ☐ Pet Friendly
☐ Store   ☐ Cafe   ☐ Firewood
☐ Ice   ☐ Security   ☐ Quiet   ☐ Noisy

☐ Antenna Reception   ☐ Satellite TV   ☐ Cable TV
☐ WIFI Available   ☐ Free   ☐ Fee $ _____

Memberships:

Amenities:

Location	☺ ☺ ☹	Water Pressure	☺ ☺ ☹
Restrooms	☺ ☺ ☹	Laundry	☺ ☺ ☹
Pool	☺ ☺ ☹	Hot Tub	☺ ☺ ☹

PLACES VISITED / ACTIVITIES:

PEOPLE MET / NEW FRIENDS:

FOOD, DINING & RESTAURANTS:

HIGHLIGHTS / MEMORABLE EVENTS:

PLACES TO GO & THINGS TO DO FOR NEXT TIME:

NOTES:

Date: _____

Weather:

☀ ☁ ☂ ❄
🌡 🌨 🎐 🌬

From: _____

To: _____

Route Taken: _____

_____

Beginning Mileage: _____

Ending Mileage: _____

Total Miles Traveled: _____

CAMPGROUND INFORMATION

Name: _____

Address: _____

Phone: _____

Our Rating: ☆ ☆ ☆ ☆ ☆

GPS: _____

Altitude: _____

Cell Service / Carrier: _____

Site # _____ $ _____ ☐ Day ☐ Week ☐ Month

☐ First Visit	☐ Return Visit	☐ Easy Access
☐ Site Level	☐ Back-in	☐ Pull-through
☐ 15 amp	☐ 30 amp	☐ 50 amp
☐ Water	☐ Sewer	☐ Shade ☐ Sun
☐ Paved	☐ Sand / Grass	☐ Gravel
☐ Picnic Table	☐ Fire ring	☐ Trees ☐ Lawn
☐ Patio	☐ Kid Friendly	☐ Pet Friendly
☐ Store	☐ Cafe	☐ Firewood
☐ Ice	☐ Security	☐ Quiet ☐ Noisy

☐ Antenna Reception ☐ Satellite TV ☐ Cable TV
☐ WIFI Available ☐ Free ☐ Fee $ _____

Memberships: _____

Amenities: _____

Location	☺ ☺ ☹	Water Pressure	☺ ☺ ☹
Restrooms	☺ ☺ ☹	Laundry	☺ ☺ ☹
Pool	☺ ☺ ☹	Hot Tub	☺ ☺ ☹

PLACES VISITED / ACTIVITIES:

_____
_____
_____
_____

PEOPLE MET / NEW FRIENDS:

_____
_____
_____
_____

FOOD, DINING & RESTAURANTS:

_____
_____
_____
_____

HIGHLIGHTS / MEMORABLE EVENTS:

_____
_____
_____
_____

PLACES TO GO & THINGS TO DO FOR NEXT TIME:

_____
_____
_____
_____
_____

NOTES:

Date: _____	From: _____	Beginning Mileage: _____
Weather:	To: _____	_____
	Route Taken: _____	Ending Mileage: _____
	_____	_____
		Total Miles Traveled: _____

Campground Information

Name: _____

Address: _____

Phone: _____

Our Rating: ☆ ☆ ☆ ☆ ☆

GPS: _____

Altitude: _____

Site # _____ **$** _____ ☐ Day ☐ Week ☐ Month

Cell Service / Carrier: _____

☐ First Visit	☐ Return Visit	☐ Easy Access
☐ Site Level	☐ Back-in	☐ Pull-through
☐ 15 amp	☐ 30 amp	☐ 50 amp
☐ Water	☐ Sewer	☐ Shade ☐ Sun
☐ Paved	☐ Sand / Grass	☐ Gravel
☐ Picnic Table	☐ Fire ring	☐ Trees ☐ Lawn
☐ Patio	☐ Kid Friendly	☐ Pet Friendly
☐ Store	☐ Cafe	☐ Firewood
☐ Ice	☐ Security	☐ Quiet ☐ Noisy

☐ Antenna Reception   ☐ Satellite TV   ☐ Cable TV

☐ WIFI Available   ☐ Free   ☐ Fee $ _____

Memberships: _____

Amenities: _____

Location	☺	☺	☹	Water Pressure	☺	☺	☹
Restrooms	☺	☺	☹	Laundry	☺	☺	☹
Pool	☺	☺	☹	Hot Tub	☺	☺	☹

Places Visited / Activities: _____

_____

_____

_____

People Met / New Friends: _____

_____

_____

_____

Food, Dining & Restaurants: _____

_____

_____

_____

Highlights / Memorable Events: _____

_____

_____

_____

Places To Go & Things To Do for Next Time: _____

_____

_____

_____

_____

NOTES:

Date: _____	From: _____	Beginning Mileage: _____
Weather:	To: _____	_____
	Route Taken: _____	Ending Mileage: _____
	_____	_____
		Total Miles Traveled: _____

CAMPGROUND INFORMATION

Name: _____

Address: _____

Phone: _____

Site # _____ $ _____ ☐ Day ☐ Week ☐ Month

☐ First Visit   ☐ Return Visit   ☐ Easy Access
☐ Site Level   ☐ Back-in   ☐ Pull-through
☐ 15 amp   ☐ 30 amp   ☐ 50 amp
☐ Water   ☐ Sewer   ☐ Shade   ☐ Sun
☐ Paved   ☐ Sand / Grass   ☐ Gravel
☐ Picnic Table   ☐ Fire ring   ☐ Trees   ☐ Lawn
☐ Patio   ☐ Kid Friendly   ☐ Pet Friendly
☐ Store   ☐ Cafe   ☐ Firewood
☐ Ice   ☐ Security   ☐ Quiet   ☐ Noisy

Our Rating: ☆ ☆ ☆ ☆ ☆

GPS: _____

Altitude: _____

Cell Service / Carrier: _____

☐ Antenna Reception   ☐ Satellite TV   ☐ Cable TV
☐ WIFI Available   ☐ Free   ☐ Fee $ _____

Memberships: _____

Amenities: _____

Location	☺	☺	☹	Water Pressure	☺ ☺ ☹
Restrooms	☺	☺	☹	Laundry	☺ ☺ ☹
Pool	☺	☺	☹	Hot Tub	☺ ☺ ☹

PLACES VISITED / ACTIVITIES:

_____

_____

_____

_____

PEOPLE MET / NEW FRIENDS:

_____

_____

_____

FOOD, DINING & RESTAURANTS:

_____

_____

_____

_____

HIGHLIGHTS / MEMORABLE EVENTS:

_____

_____

_____

_____

PLACES TO GO & THINGS TO DO FOR NEXT TIME:

_____

_____

_____

_____

NOTES: _____

Date: _____

Weather:

☀ ☁ ☂ ❄

🌡 🌡 📢 🌩

From: _____

To: _____

Route Taken: _____

_____

Beginning Mileage: _____

Ending Mileage: _____

Total Miles Traveled: _____

CAMPGROUND INFORMATION

Name: _____

Address: _____

Phone: _____

Site # _____ $ _____ ☐ Day ☐ Week ☐ Month

☐ First Visit	☐ Return Visit	☐ Easy Access	
☐ Site Level	☐ Back-in	☐ Pull-through	
☐ 15 amp	☐ 30 amp	☐ 50 amp	
☐ Water	☐ Sewer	☐ Shade	☐ Sun
☐ Paved	☐ Sand / Grass	☐ Gravel	
☐ Picnic Table	☐ Fire ring	☐ Trees	☐ Lawn
☐ Patio	☐ Kid Friendly	☐ Pet Friendly	
☐ Store	☐ Cafe	☐ Firewood	
☐ Ice	☐ Security	☐ Quiet	☐ Noisy

Our Rating: ☆ ☆ ☆ ☆ ☆

GPS: _____

Altitude: _____

Cell Service / Carrier: _____

☐ Antenna Reception ☐ Satellite TV ☐ Cable TV

☐ WIFI Available ☐ Free ☐ Fee $ _____

Memberships: _____

Amenities: _____

Location	☺ ☹ ☹	Water Pressure	☺ ☹ ☹
Restrooms	☺ ☹ ☹	Laundry	☺ ☹ ☹
Pool	☺ ☹ ☹	Hot Tub	☺ ☹ ☹

PLACES VISITED / ACTIVITIES: _____

_____

_____

_____

PEOPLE MET / NEW FRIENDS: _____

_____

_____

_____

FOOD, DINING & RESTAURANTS: _____

_____

_____

_____

HIGHLIGHTS / MEMORABLE EVENTS: _____

_____

_____

_____

PLACES TO GO & THINGS TO DO FOR NEXT TIME: _____

_____

_____

_____

_____

NOTES:

Date: _____	From: _____	Beginning Mileage: _____
Weather:	To: _____	
☀ ☁ ☂ ❄	Route Taken: _____	Ending Mileage: _____
🌡 🌡❄ 🎐 ☁	_____	Total Miles Traveled: _____

CAMPGROUND INFORMATION

Name: _____   Our Rating: ☆ ☆ ☆ ☆ ☆

Address: _____   GPS: _____

Phone: _____   Altitude: _____

Site # _____ $ _____   Cell Service / Carrier: _____

☐ Day ☐ Week ☐ Month

☐ First Visit	☐ Return Visit	☐ Easy Access
☐ Site Level	☐ Back-in	☐ Pull-through
☐ 15 amp	☐ 30 amp	☐ 50 amp
☐ Water	☐ Sewer	☐ Shade ☐ Sun
☐ Paved	☐ Sand / Grass	☐ Gravel
☐ Picnic Table	☐ Fire ring	☐ Trees ☐ Lawn
☐ Patio	☐ Kid Friendly	☐ Pet Friendly
☐ Store	☐ Cafe	☐ Firewood
☐ Ice	☐ Security	☐ Quiet ☐ Noisy

☐ Antenna Reception   ☐ Satellite TV   ☐ Cable TV
☐ WIFI Available   ☐ Free ☐ Fee $ _____

Memberships: _____

Amenities: _____

Location	☺ ☺ ☹	Water Pressure	☺ ☺ ☹
Restrooms	☺ ☺ ☹	Laundry	☺ ☺ ☹
Pool	☺ ☺ ☹	Hot Tub	☺ ☺ ☹

PLACES VISITED / ACTIVITIES: _____
_____
_____
_____

PEOPLE MET / NEW FRIENDS: _____
_____
_____
_____

FOOD, DINING & RESTAURANTS: _____
_____
_____
_____

HIGHLIGHTS / MEMORABLE EVENTS: _____
_____
_____
_____

PLACES TO GO & THINGS TO DO FOR NEXT TIME: _____
_____
_____
_____
_____

NOTES:

Date: _____

Weather:

☀ ⛅ ☂ ❄
🌡 ❄🌡 🎌 ☁

From: _____

To: _____

Route Taken: _____

_____

Beginning Mileage: _____

_____

Ending Mileage: _____

_____

Total Miles Traveled: _____

CAMPGROUND INFORMATION

Name: _____

Address: _____

Phone: _____

Site # _____ $ _____ ☐ Day ☐ Week ☐ Month

☐ First Visit   ☐ Return Visit   ☐ Easy Access
☐ Site Level   ☐ Back-in   ☐ Pull-through
☐ 15 amp   ☐ 30 amp   ☐ 50 amp
☐ Water   ☐ Sewer   ☐ Shade   ☐ Sun
☐ Paved   ☐ Sand / Grass   ☐ Gravel
☐ Picnic Table   ☐ Fire ring   ☐ Trees   ☐ Lawn
☐ Patio   ☐ Kid Friendly   ☐ Pet Friendly
☐ Store   ☐ Cafe   ☐ Firewood
☐ Ice   ☐ Security   ☐ Quiet   ☐ Noisy

Our Rating: ☆ ☆ ☆ ☆ ☆

GPS: _____

Altitude: _____

Cell Service / Carrier: _____

☐ Antenna Reception   ☐ Satellite TV   ☐ Cable TV
☐ WIFI Available   ☐ Free ☐ Fee $ _____

Memberships: _____

Amenities: _____

Location	☺	😐	☹	Water Pressure	☺	😐	☹
Restrooms	☺	😐	☹	Laundry	☺	😐	☹
Pool	☺	😐	☹	Hot Tub	☺	😐	☹

PLACES VISITED / ACTIVITIES: _____

_____

_____

_____

PEOPLE MET / NEW FRIENDS: _____

_____

_____

_____

FOOD, DINING & RESTAURANTS: _____

_____

_____

_____

HIGHLIGHTS / MEMORABLE EVENTS: _____

_____

_____

_____

PLACES TO GO & THINGS TO DO FOR NEXT TIME: _____

_____

_____

_____

_____

NOTES:

Date: _____	From: _____	Beginning Mileage:
	To: _____	_____
Weather:	Route Taken: _____	Ending Mileage:
☀ ☁ ☂ ❄	_____	_____
🌡 🌡❄ 🎏 ☁		Total Miles Traveled:

CAMPGROUND INFORMATION

Name: _____	Our Rating: ☆ ☆ ☆ ☆ ☆
Address: _____	GPS: _____
Phone: _____	Altitude: _____

Site # _____ $ _____ ☐ Day ☐ Week ☐ Month

Cell Service / Carrier: _____

☐ First Visit	☐ Return Visit	☐ Easy Access
☐ Site Level	☐ Back-in	☐ Pull-through
☐ 15 amp	☐ 30 amp	☐ 50 amp
☐ Water	☐ Sewer	☐ Shade ☐ Sun
☐ Paved	☐ Sand / Grass	☐ Gravel
☐ Picnic Table	☐ Fire ring	☐ Trees ☐ Lawn
☐ Patio	☐ Kid Friendly	☐ Pet Friendly
☐ Store	☐ Cafe	☐ Firewood
☐ Ice	☐ Security	☐ Quiet ☐ Noisy

☐ Antenna Reception ☐ Satellite TV ☐ Cable TV
☐ WIFI Available ☐ Free ☐ Fee $ _____

Memberships: _____
Amenities: _____

Location	☺ ☺ ☹	Water Pressure	☺ ☺ ☹
Restrooms	☺ ☺ ☹	Laundry	☺ ☺ ☹
Pool	☺ ☺ ☹	Hot Tub	☺ ☺ ☹

PLACES VISITED / ACTIVITIES: _____

_____
_____
_____

PEOPLE MET / NEW FRIENDS: _____

_____
_____
_____

FOOD, DINING & RESTAURANTS: _____

_____
_____
_____

HIGHLIGHTS / MEMORABLE EVENTS: _____

_____
_____
_____

PLACES TO GO & THINGS TO DO FOR NEXT TIME: _____

_____
_____
_____
_____

NOTES:

Date: _____	From: _____	Beginning Mileage:
	To: _____	_____
Weather:		Ending Mileage:
☀ ☁ ☂ ❄	Route Taken: _____	_____
🌡 ❄🌡 🚩 ☁	_____	Total Miles Traveled:

CAMPGROUND INFORMATION

Name: _____

Our Rating: ☆ ☆ ☆ ☆ ☆

Address: _____

GPS: _____

Phone: _____

Altitude: _____

Site # _____ $ _____ ☐ Day ☐ Week ☐ Month

Cell Service / Carrier: _____

☐ First Visit ☐ Return Visit ☐ Easy Access

☐ Antenna Reception ☐ Satellite TV ☐ Cable TV

☐ Site Level ☐ Back-in ☐ Pull-through

☐ WIFI Available ☐ Free ☐ Fee $ _____

☐ 15 amp ☐ 30 amp ☐ 50 amp

☐ Water ☐ Sewer ☐ Shade ☐ Sun

Memberships: _____

☐ Paved ☐ Sand / Grass ☐ Gravel

Amenities: _____

☐ Picnic Table ☐ Fire ring ☐ Trees ☐ Lawn

Location ☺ ☺ ☹ Water Pressure ☺ ☺ ☹

☐ Patio ☐ Kid Friendly ☐ Pet Friendly

Restrooms ☺ ☺ ☹ Laundry ☺ ☺ ☹

☐ Store ☐ Cafe ☐ Firewood

Pool ☺ ☺ ☹ Hot Tub ☺ ☺ ☹

☐ Ice ☐ Security ☐ Quiet ☐ Noisy

PLACES VISITED / ACTIVITIES: _____

_____
_____
_____
_____

PEOPLE MET / NEW FRIENDS: _____

_____
_____
_____
_____

FOOD, DINING & RESTAURANTS: _____

_____
_____
_____
_____

HIGHLIGHTS / MEMORABLE EVENTS: _____

_____
_____
_____

PLACES TO GO & THINGS TO DO FOR NEXT TIME: _____

_____
_____
_____
_____

NOTES:

Date: _____

Weather:

☀ ⛅ ☔ ❄
🌡 🌡 🔦 ☁

From: _____

To: _____

Route Taken: _____

_____

Beginning Mileage: _____

_____

Ending Mileage: _____

_____

Total Miles Traveled: _____

CAMPGROUND INFORMATION

Name: _____

Address: _____

Phone: _____

Site # _____ $ _____

☐ First Visit
☐ Site Level
☐ 15 amp
☐ Water
☐ Paved
☐ Picnic Table
☐ Patio
☐ Store
☐ Ice

☐ Return Visit
☐ Back-in
☐ 30 amp
☐ Sewer
☐ Sand / Grass
☐ Fire ring
☐ Kid Friendly
☐ Cafe
☐ Security

☐ Day ☐ Week ☐ Month

☐ Easy Access
☐ Pull-through
☐ 50 amp
☐ Shade ☐ Sun
☐ Gravel
☐ Trees ☐ Lawn
☐ Pet Friendly
☐ Firewood
☐ Quiet ☐ Noisy

Our Rating: ☆ ☆ ☆ ☆ ☆

GPS: _____

Altitude: _____

Cell Service / Carrier: _____

☐ Antenna Reception   ☐ Satellite TV   ☐ Cable TV
☐ WIFI Available   ☐ Free ☐ Fee $ _____

Memberships: _____

Amenities: _____

Location	☺	😐	☹	Water Pressure	☺	😐	☹
Restrooms	☺	😐	☹	Laundry	☺	😐	☹
Pool	☺	😐	☹	Hot Tub	☺	😐	☹

PLACES VISITED / ACTIVITIES: _____

_____

_____

_____

PEOPLE MET / NEW FRIENDS: _____

_____

_____

_____

FOOD, DINING & RESTAURANTS: _____

_____

_____

_____

HIGHLIGHTS / MEMORABLE EVENTS: _____

_____

_____

_____

PLACES TO GO & THINGS TO DO FOR NEXT TIME: _____

_____

_____

_____

_____

NOTES:

Date: _____

Weather:

From: _____

To: _____

Route Taken: _____
_____

Beginning Mileage: _____

Ending Mileage: _____

Total Miles Traveled: _____

CAMPGROUND INFORMATION

Name: _____

Address: _____

Phone: _____

Site # _____ $ _____

☐ Day ☐ Week ☐ Month

☐ First Visit   ☐ Return Visit   ☐ Easy Access
☐ Site Level   ☐ Back-in   ☐ Pull-through
☐ 15 amp   ☐ 30 amp   ☐ 50 amp
☐ Water   ☐ Sewer   ☐ Shade   ☐ Sun
☐ Paved   ☐ Sand / Grass   ☐ Gravel
☐ Picnic Table   ☐ Fire ring   ☐ Trees   ☐ Lawn
☐ Patio   ☐ Kid Friendly   ☐ Pet Friendly
☐ Store   ☐ Cafe   ☐ Firewood
☐ Ice   ☐ Security   ☐ Quiet   ☐ Noisy

Our Rating: ☆ ☆ ☆ ☆ ☆

GPS: _____

Altitude: _____

Cell Service / Carrier: _____

☐ Antenna Reception   ☐ Satellite TV   ☐ Cable TV
☐ WIFI Available   ☐ Free ☐ Fee $ _____

Memberships: _____

Amenities: _____

Location	☺	😐	☹	Water Pressure	☺	😐	☹
Restrooms	☺	😐	☹	Laundry	☺	😐	☹
Pool	☺	😐	☹	Hot Tub	☺	😐	☹

PLACES VISITED / ACTIVITIES: _____
_____
_____
_____

PEOPLE MET / NEW FRIENDS: _____
_____
_____
_____

FOOD, DINING & RESTAURANTS: _____
_____
_____
_____

HIGHLIGHTS / MEMORABLE EVENTS: _____
_____
_____
_____

PLACES TO GO & THINGS TO DO FOR NEXT TIME: _____
_____
_____
_____
_____

NOTES:

Date: _____

Weather:

From: _____
To: _____
Route Taken: _____
_____

Beginning Mileage: _____

Ending Mileage: _____

Total Miles Traveled: _____

CAMPGROUND INFORMATION

Name: _____

Address: _____

Phone: _____

Site # _____ $ _____   ☐ Day ☐ Week ☐ Month

☐ First Visit   ☐ Return Visit   ☐ Easy Access
☐ Site Level   ☐ Back-in   ☐ Pull-through
☐ 15 amp   ☐ 30 amp   ☐ 50 amp
☐ Water   ☐ Sewer   ☐ Shade   ☐ Sun
☐ Paved   ☐ Sand / Grass   ☐ Gravel
☐ Picnic Table   ☐ Fire ring   ☐ Trees   ☐ Lawn
☐ Patio   ☐ Kid Friendly   ☐ Pet Friendly
☐ Store   ☐ Cafe   ☐ Firewood
☐ Ice   ☐ Security   ☐ Quiet   ☐ Noisy

Our Rating: ☆ ☆ ☆ ☆ ☆

GPS: _____

Altitude: _____

Cell Service / Carrier: _____

☐ Antenna Reception   ☐ Satellite TV   ☐ Cable TV
☐ WIFI Available   ☐ Free ☐ Fee $ _____

Memberships: _____

Amenities:

Location	☺ ☺ ☹	Water Pressure	☺ ☺ ☹
Restrooms	☺ ☺ ☹	Laundry	☺ ☺ ☹
Pool	☺ ☺ ☹	Hot Tub	☺ ☺ ☹

PLACES VISITED / ACTIVITIES: _____
_____
_____
_____

PEOPLE MET / NEW FRIENDS: _____
_____
_____
_____

FOOD, DINING & RESTAURANTS: _____
_____
_____
_____

HIGHLIGHTS / MEMORABLE EVENTS: _____
_____
_____
_____

PLACES TO GO & THINGS TO DO FOR NEXT TIME: _____
_____
_____
_____
_____

NOTES:

Date: _____

Weather:

From: _____

To: _____

Route Taken: _____

_____

Beginning Mileage: _____

Ending Mileage: _____

Total Miles Traveled: _____

CAMPGROUND INFORMATION

Name: _____

Address: _____

Phone: _____

Site # _____ $ _____ ☐ Day ☐ Week ☐ Month

☐ First Visit
☐ Site Level
☐ 15 amp
☐ Water
☐ Paved
☐ Picnic Table
☐ Patio
☐ Store
☐ Ice

☐ Return Visit
☐ Back-in
☐ 30 amp
☐ Sewer
☐ Sand / Grass
☐ Fire ring
☐ Kid Friendly
☐ Cafe
☐ Security

☐ Easy Access
☐ Pull-through
☐ 50 amp
☐ Shade
☐ Gravel
☐ Trees
☐ Pet Friendly
☐ Firewood
☐ Quiet

☐ Sun

☐ Lawn

☐ Noisy

Our Rating: ☆ ☆ ☆ ☆ ☆

GPS: _____

Altitude: _____

Cell Service / Carrier: _____

☐ Antenna Reception   ☐ Satellite TV   ☐ Cable TV
☐ WIFI Available   ☐ Free ☐ Fee $ _____

Memberships: _____

Amenities: _____

Location	☺	☻	☹	Water Pressure	☺	☻	☹
Restrooms	☺	☻	☹	Laundry	☺	☻	☹
Pool	☺	☻	☹	Hot Tub	☺	☻	☹

PLACES VISITED / ACTIVITIES: _____

_____

_____

_____

PEOPLE MET / NEW FRIENDS: _____

_____

_____

_____

FOOD, DINING & RESTAURANTS: _____

_____

_____

_____

HIGHLIGHTS / MEMORABLE EVENTS: _____

_____

_____

_____

PLACES TO GO & THINGS TO DO FOR NEXT TIME: _____

_____

_____

_____

_____

NOTES:

Date: _____

Weather:

From: _____

To: _____

Route Taken: _____

_____

Beginning Mileage: _____

Ending Mileage: _____

Total Miles Traveled: _____

CAMPGROUND INFORMATION

Name: _____

Address: _____

Phone: _____

Site # _____ $ _____

☐ Day ☐ Week ☐ Month

☐ First Visit
☐ Site Level
☐ 15 amp
☐ Water
☐ Paved
☐ Picnic Table
☐ Patio
☐ Store
☐ Ice

☐ Return Visit
☐ Back-in
☐ 30 amp
☐ Sewer
☐ Sand / Grass
☐ Fire ring
☐ Kid Friendly
☐ Cafe
☐ Security

☐ Easy Access
☐ Pull-through
☐ 50 amp
☐ Shade   ☐ Sun
☐ Gravel
☐ Trees   ☐ Lawn
☐ Pet Friendly
☐ Firewood
☐ Quiet   ☐ Noisy

Our Rating: ☆ ☆ ☆ ☆ ☆

GPS: _____

Altitude: _____

Cell Service / Carrier: _____

☐ Antenna Reception   ☐ Satellite TV   ☐ Cable TV
☐ WIFI Available   ☐ Free ☐ Fee $ _____

Memberships: _____

Amenities: _____

Location	☺	😐	☹	Water Pressure	☺	😐	☹
Restrooms	☺	😐	☹	Laundry	☺	😐	☹
Pool	☺	😐	☹	Hot Tub	☺	😐	☹

PLACES VISITED / ACTIVITIES: _____

_____

_____

_____

PEOPLE MET / NEW FRIENDS: _____

_____

_____

_____

FOOD, DINING & RESTAURANTS: _____

_____

_____

_____

HIGHLIGHTS / MEMORABLE EVENTS: _____

_____

_____

_____

PLACES TO GO & THINGS TO DO FOR NEXT TIME: _____

_____

_____

_____

_____

NOTES:

Date: _____

Weather:

☀ ☁ ☂ ❄

🌡 ❄🌡 🚩 ☁

From: _____

To: _____

Route Taken: _____

_____

Beginning Mileage: _____

_____

Ending Mileage: _____

_____

Total Miles Traveled: _____

CAMPGROUND INFORMATION

Name: _____

Address: _____

Phone: _____

Site # _____ $ _____

☐ First Visit ☐ Return Visit ☐ Day ☐ Week ☐ Month

☐ First Visit ☐ Return Visit ☐ Easy Access
☐ Site Level ☐ Back-in ☐ Pull-through
☐ 15 amp ☐ 30 amp ☐ 50 amp
☐ Water ☐ Sewer ☐ Shade ☐ Sun
☐ Paved ☐ Sand / Grass ☐ Gravel
☐ Picnic Table ☐ Fire ring ☐ Trees ☐ Lawn
☐ Patio ☐ Kid Friendly ☐ Pet Friendly
☐ Store ☐ Cafe ☐ Firewood
☐ Ice ☐ Security ☐ Quiet ☐ Noisy

Our Rating: ☆ ☆ ☆ ☆ ☆

GPS: _____

Altitude: _____

Cell Service / Carrier: _____

☐ Antenna Reception ☐ Satellite TV ☐ Cable TV
☐ WIFI Available ☐ Free ☐ Fee $ _____

Memberships: _____

Amenities: _____

Location	☺	☻	☹	Water Pressure	☺	☻	☹
Restrooms	☺	☻	☹	Laundry	☺	☻	☹
Pool	☺	☻	☹	Hot Tub	☺	☻	☹

PLACES VISITED / ACTIVITIES: _____

_____

_____

_____

PEOPLE MET / NEW FRIENDS: _____

_____

_____

_____

FOOD, DINING & RESTAURANTS: _____

_____

_____

_____

HIGHLIGHTS / MEMORABLE EVENTS: _____

_____

_____

_____

PLACES TO GO & THINGS TO DO FOR NEXT TIME: _____

_____

_____

_____

_____

NOTES:

Date: _____	From: _____	Beginning Mileage:
Weather:	To: _____	_____
☀ ⛅ ☂ ❄	Route Taken: _____	Ending Mileage:
🌡 ❄ 🚩 ☁	_____	_____
		Total Miles Traveled:

CAMPGROUND INFORMATION

Name: _____	Our Rating: ☆ ☆ ☆ ☆ ☆
Address: _____	GPS: _____
Phone: _____	Altitude: _____

Site # _____ $ _____ ☐ Day ☐ Week ☐ Month

Cell Service / Carrier: _____

☐ First Visit   ☐ Return Visit   ☐ Easy Access
☐ Site Level   ☐ Back-in   ☐ Pull-through
☐ 15 amp   ☐ 30 amp   ☐ 50 amp
☐ Water   ☐ Sewer   ☐ Shade   ☐ Sun
☐ Paved   ☐ Sand / Grass   ☐ Gravel
☐ Picnic Table   ☐ Fire ring   ☐ Trees   ☐ Lawn
☐ Patio   ☐ Kid Friendly   ☐ Pet Friendly
☐ Store   ☐ Cafe   ☐ Firewood
☐ Ice   ☐ Security   ☐ Quiet   ☐ Noisy

☐ Antenna Reception   ☐ Satellite TV   ☐ Cable TV
☐ WIFI Available   ☐ Free   ☐ Fee $ _____

Memberships: _____

Amenities: _____

Location	☺	😐	☹	Water Pressure	☺ 😐 ☹
Restrooms	☺	😐	☹	Laundry	☺ 😐 ☹
Pool	☺	😐	☹	Hot Tub	☺ 😐 ☹

PLACES VISITED / ACTIVITIES: _____
_____
_____
_____

PEOPLE MET / NEW FRIENDS: _____
_____
_____
_____

FOOD, DINING & RESTAURANTS: _____
_____
_____
_____

HIGHLIGHTS / MEMORABLE EVENTS: _____
_____
_____
_____

PLACES TO GO & THINGS TO DO FOR NEXT TIME: _____
_____
_____
_____
_____

NOTES:

Date: _____

Weather:

☀ ☁ ☔ ❄
🌡 🌡❄ 🎐 ☁

From: _____

To: _____

Route Taken: _____
_____

Beginning Mileage: _____

Ending Mileage: _____

Total Miles Traveled: _____

CAMPGROUND INFORMATION

Name: _____

Address: _____

Phone: _____

Site # _____ $ _____ ☐ Day ☐ Week ☐ Month

☐ First Visit   ☐ Return Visit   ☐ Easy Access
☐ Site Level   ☐ Back-in   ☐ Pull-through
☐ 15 amp   ☐ 30 amp   ☐ 50 amp
☐ Water   ☐ Sewer   ☐ Shade   ☐ Sun
☐ Paved   ☐ Sand / Grass   ☐ Gravel
☐ Picnic Table   ☐ Fire ring   ☐ Trees   ☐ Lawn
☐ Patio   ☐ Kid Friendly   ☐ Pet Friendly
☐ Store   ☐ Cafe   ☐ Firewood
☐ Ice   ☐ Security   ☐ Quiet   ☐ Noisy

Our Rating: ☆ ☆ ☆ ☆ ☆

GPS: _____

Altitude: _____

Cell Service / Carrier: _____

☐ Antenna Reception   ☐ Satellite TV   ☐ Cable TV
☐ WIFI Available   ☐ Free ☐ Fee $ _____

Memberships: _____

Amenities: _____

Location	☺	😐	☹	Water Pressure	☺	😐	☹
Restrooms	☺	😐	☹	Laundry	☺	😐	☹
Pool	☺	😐	☹	Hot Tub	☺	😐	☹

PLACES VISITED / ACTIVITIES: _____
_____
_____
_____
_____

PEOPLE MET / NEW FRIENDS: _____
_____
_____
_____
_____

FOOD, DINING & RESTAURANTS: _____
_____
_____
_____

HIGHLIGHTS / MEMORABLE EVENTS: _____
_____
_____
_____
_____

PLACES TO GO & THINGS TO DO FOR NEXT TIME: _____
_____
_____
_____
_____

NOTES:

Date:	From:	Beginning Mileage:
Weather:	To:	Ending Mileage:
	Route Taken:	Total Miles Traveled:

Campground Information

Name:

Address:

Phone:

Site # _____ $ _____ ☐ Day ☐ Week ☐ Month

☐ First Visit ☐ Return Visit ☐ Easy Access
☐ Site Level ☐ Back-in ☐ Pull-through
☐ 15 amp ☐ 30 amp ☐ 50 amp
☐ Water ☐ Sewer ☐ Shade ☐ Sun
☐ Paved ☐ Sand / Grass ☐ Gravel
☐ Picnic Table ☐ Fire ring ☐ Trees ☐ Lawn
☐ Patio ☐ Kid Friendly ☐ Pet Friendly
☐ Store ☐ Cafe ☐ Firewood
☐ Ice ☐ Security ☐ Quiet ☐ Noisy

Our Rating: ☆ ☆ ☆ ☆ ☆

GPS:

Altitude:

Cell Service / Carrier:

☐ Antenna Reception ☐ Satellite TV ☐ Cable TV
☐ WIFI Available ☐ Free ☐ Fee $ _____

Memberships:

Amenities:

Location	☺ ☻ ☹	Water Pressure	☺ ☻ ☹
Restrooms	☺ ☻ ☹	Laundry	☺ ☻ ☹
Pool	☺ ☻ ☹	Hot Tub	☺ ☻ ☹

Places Visited / Activities:

People Met / New Friends:

Food, Dining & Restaurants:

Highlights / Memorable Events:

Places To Go & Things To Do for Next Time:

NOTES:

Date: _____	From: _____	Beginning Mileage:
Weather:	To: _____	_____
	Route Taken: _____	Ending Mileage:
	_____	_____
		Total Miles Traveled:

Campground Information

Name: _____

Address: _____

Phone: _____

Site # _____ $ _____ ☐ Day ☐ Week ☐ Month

☐ First Visit ☐ Return Visit ☐ Easy Access
☐ Site Level ☐ Back-in ☐ Pull-through
☐ 15 amp ☐ 30 amp ☐ 50 amp
☐ Water ☐ Sewer ☐ Shade ☐ Sun
☐ Paved ☐ Sand / Grass ☐ Gravel
☐ Picnic Table ☐ Fire ring ☐ Trees ☐ Lawn
☐ Patio ☐ Kid Friendly ☐ Pet Friendly
☐ Store ☐ Cafe ☐ Firewood
☐ Ice ☐ Security ☐ Quiet ☐ Noisy

Our Rating: ☆ ☆ ☆ ☆ ☆

GPS: _____

Altitude: _____

Cell Service / Carrier: _____

☐ Antenna Reception ☐ Satellite TV ☐ Cable TV
☐ WIFI Available ☐ Free ☐ Fee $ _____

Memberships: _____

Amenities: _____

Location	☺ ☺ ☹	Water Pressure	☺ ☺ ☹
Restrooms	☺ ☺ ☹	Laundry	☺ ☺ ☹
Pool	☺ ☺ ☹	Hot Tub	☺ ☺ ☹

Places Visited / Activities: _____

_____
_____
_____

People Met / New Friends: _____

_____
_____
_____

Food, Dining & Restaurants: _____

_____
_____
_____

Highlights / Memorable Events: _____

_____
_____
_____

Places To Go & Things To Do for Next Time: _____

_____
_____
_____
_____

NOTES:

Date: _____	From: _____	Beginning Mileage: _____
	To: _____	Ending Mileage: _____
Weather: ☀ ⛅ ☂ ❄ 🌡 🌡 🚩 ☁	Route Taken: _____ _____	Total Miles Traveled: _____

Campground Information

Name: _____	Our Rating: ☆ ☆ ☆ ☆ ☆
Address: _____	GPS: _____
Phone: _____	Altitude: _____
Site # _____ $ _____ ☐ Day ☐ Week ☐ Month	Cell Service / Carrier: _____

Site #: ☐ First Visit ☐ Return Visit ☐ Easy Access
☐ Site Level ☐ Back-in ☐ Pull-through
☐ 15 amp ☐ 30 amp ☐ 50 amp
☐ Water ☐ Sewer ☐ Shade ☐ Sun
☐ Paved ☐ Sand / Grass ☐ Gravel
☐ Picnic Table ☐ Fire ring ☐ Trees ☐ Lawn
☐ Patio ☐ Kid Friendly ☐ Pet Friendly
☐ Store ☐ Cafe ☐ Firewood
☐ Ice ☐ Security ☐ Quiet ☐ Noisy

☐ Antenna Reception ☐ Satellite TV ☐ Cable TV
☐ WIFI Available ☐ Free ☐ Fee $ _____
Memberships: _____
Amenities: _____

Location	☺	☺	☹	Water Pressure	☺	☺	☹
Restrooms	☺	☺	☹	Laundry	☺	☺	☹
Pool	☺	☺	☹	Hot Tub	☺	☺	☹

Places Visited / Activities: _____

_____
_____
_____

People Met / New Friends: _____

_____
_____
_____

Food, Dining & Restaurants: _____

_____
_____
_____

Highlights / Memorable Events: _____

_____
_____
_____

Places To Go & Things To Do for Next Time: _____

_____
_____
_____
_____

NOTES:

Made in the USA
Las Vegas, NV
18 December 2022

63338965R00090